Author of 14 books, including

THE LOCKET
GRAPES OF GLORY
MY COPE RUNNETH OVER
RAINBOW OF PROMISE

Tales of the Endless Mountains

A TRUE STORY OF MIDWEST CITY SLICKERS LEARNING
LOVE AND PATIENCE IN A MOUNTAIN HAMLET

Adell Farley Harvey

WESTBOW
PRESS
A DIVISION OF THOMAS NELSON

WestBow Press books may be ordered through booksellers or by contacting:

WestBow Press
A Division of Thomas Nelson
1663 Liberty Drive
Bloomington, IN 47403
www.westbowpress.com
1-(866) 928-1240

ISBN: 978-1-4497-1766-7 (sc)
ISBN: 978-1-4497-1767-4 (hc)
ISBN: 978-1-4497-1765-0 (e)

Library of Congress Control Number: 2011929582

Printed in the United States of America

WestBow Press rev. date: 06/01/2011

For Billy, Mari, and Jeff—to help you become
better acquainted with your birth Daddy

The Saga of the Missionary Lark

Some trust in chariots, and some in horses: but we will
remember the name of the LORD our God. Ps. 20:7

In 1964, my young husband and I answered God's call to serve in a rural mission field in northern Appalachia. Armed with little more than a great confidence in God, we bumbled our way through culture shock, church problems, and health issues. Emboldened by the arrogance of youth, we loaded ourselves down with pastoral duties, went where "angels fear to tread," and tackled problems that would have made spiritual giants tremble.

Perhaps to cover up our lack of insight and experience, we determined never to gripe or to complain to our mountain congregation or neighbors. We would simply trust God to get the job done. I wrote weekly letters to my mom and Bill's folks, detailing all our experiences. Both of them kept every letter we sent during those three years. Now, from the vantage point of hindsight, we easily can see where we "unloaded" all our frustrations. Letters to my mom, especially, read like a habitual whining session, where I dumped all my hurts and complaints on her—things I couldn't relate to anyone else.

Re-reading the letters I wrote so long ago gave me a fresh perspective on those fateful years, brought back memories long forgotten, and prompted me to write this book. The letters provided me a weekly journal, written as events occurred, assuring the accuracy of our recollections of experiences, emotions, and sentiments.

As faith missionaries, we sent a newsletter every month to thank our supporters, telling them how God was working among the people God had called us to serve. Both of our mothers kept those monthly letters as well.

En route to our field in the Endless Mountains, I kept a notebook handy and wrote about our experiences along the way. Just for fun, the kids and I wrote our journal entries from the viewpoint of our little car Puny. Rushed for time when we finally arrived, we decided to use the journal of our trip for our first prayer letter.

We never dreamed how popular Puny would become. He received encouragement cards, spark plugs, gift cards for engine tune-ups, even Christmas gifts. Later, on a deputation trip back to Illinois, Bethany Baptist Church put a spray of flowers on his hood, threw a "welcome home, Puny" party for him, and baked him a specially decorated car cake. Puny became our spokesman for the next several years. And "The Saga of the Missionary Lark" evolved into "The Perils of Puny."

Here's the letter that started it all:

I'm just a little blue 1963 six-cylinder Studebaker Lark. Since my owners call me "Puny," I about burst with pride when they asked me if I could pull a 5 x 8 trailer to Pennsylvania! Here was my chance to show them I wasn't so "puny" after all!

When they backed me up to that big trailer, though, I'll admit I shook clear down to my innertubes. Boy, that old gray and orange trailer was huge, and he didn't look a bit friendly either. He wasn't about to be pulled by a little fellow like me. But the laugh was on him when they started loading him up. I just stood there gurgling my carburetor and listening to him groan. When that 300-pound barrel of books hit his axles, he really complained. And I almost exploded my radiator when they had that old smart-alecky fellow as full as they could get him…and still had a porch full of boxes to go in. He wasn't as great as he thought he was.

Of course, my owners didn't think it was so funny. They needed all that stuff on the porch.

Then it was his turn to laugh when they hitched me up. I grunted and I groaned and put all my horses to work, but even so, he just about yanked my back bumper off. It was obvious I couldn't pull him out of the yard, let alone clear to Pennsylvania.

Well, the Farleys (they're my owners) went into the house and prayed for a while, then decided to let God do the worrying. That was surely some weekend. I heard all kinds of rumors that they were going to trade me on a pickup truck (and after all my months of faithful service!). Then somebody said they knew of somebody going to Pennsylvania who would gladly pull the trailer. The Farleys looked in to it, but Mr. Farley, bless his heart, said he thought I could pull the trailer as good as that old station wagon. Maybe he does appreciate me after all!

Meanwhile the trailer wasn't resting in any garden of roses either. It seems somebody wanted the bunkbeds that were already loaded on him, so they had to unload him, take off the beds, and reload again. Incidentally, that gave him enough room to carry the stuff on the porch. Then the trailer was pretty glad, too, when they sold the last bike. He was going to have to carry it on his roof! And if you've ever carried a bike on your roof, you know that can get pretty miserable.

Anyway, on Monday they bought a new trailer hitch and attached it to my frame—one the trailer couldn't yank off. So when we were hooked together this time we decided, since we were in this thing together, we might as well call a truce and cooperate. So off we went — PENNSYLVANIA OR BUST!

As mile after mile went by, we really began to click. I made a few noises that kind of worried my owners, but actually, I was just spitting and sputting happily at how well I was doing. In fact by Monday night, we were well into Ohio.

Things got a little harder on Tuesday as we got into something they called "foothills." If these were foothills, I'd hate to climb the rest of the leg!

When we finally crossed the line into Pennsylvania, you should have heard the excitement! You'd have thought we were the '49ers reaching California, or something!

At first, that mountain air had all six of my cylinders perking first rate, but as those "hills" got higher and higher, I started to have my "druthers." When the mountain summits reached two thousand feet and more, I had to use all my horses and all my gears to get over the top. Each time I'd think, "I'll never make it." Then I'd hear the kids chanting, "I think he can, I think he can," and over the top we'd go! On the way down, I'd join in, "I knew I could, I knew I could."

Just as we turned the corner onto Saco Road (that's our road), that nasty trailer gave a mean lurch, as though to remind me that the load was still there. Spitefully, he tore loose from my overloaded springs. But I hadn't come that far to be shown up like that, so I gathered all my strength for one final effort and limped on in home.

Home! What a wonderful word! They backed us up to the door, unhitched the trailer (was I ever glad to get rid of him!) and then let me rest in the garage. And did I ever need a rest!

We added a moral to the story at the end of Puny's tale of woe. *The moral of our story is two-fold. Even an underpowered "Lark" can get the job done if God is in control. Likewise, God can use ordinary missionary families like us if they yield to Him. Please pray for us!* Sadly for Puny, his rest was short-lived.

* * *

Wit-n-wisdom: God doesn't call the qualified; He qualifies the called.

Time's A Wasting!

The minute hand on the clock in the surgery waiting room lingered, suspended, then slowly lumbered on to the next dot on the clock. One minute, two minutes, three minutes, four minutes, and finally five minutes were pushed into the archives of history. Minute after painful minute ticked by, slowly but surely taking the hours with them.

It seemed my entire life had hung like that clock, suspended, ticking slowly on, waiting for this day, the day Bill's heart surgery would be history and we could get on with our plans to serve the Lord.

The first hint of a shadow crossed our lives in 1955 when we went to the local doctor for our required premarital blood tests. As Dr. Kaufman drew my blood, she gave me a gentle but frightening warning: "I hope you've weighed all the consequences, my dear. Bill has a very serious heart condition, and I'm afraid the stresses and strains of marriage will prove too much for him."

I felt a momentary pang of alarm, then dismissed the elderly doctor's warning. With my fresh-out-of-high-school optimism and enthusiasm, I pooh-poohed her comments as those of an excessive worrywart. I knew all about Bill's little heart murmur caused by rheumatic fever, but one glance at my husky, 180-pound fiancé would show anybody how healthy he was. Football player, all-around athlete—there wasn't much he couldn't accomplish.

Besides, hadn't God called Bill to preach in a very dramatic way just a couple of months earlier? Seated in the front row at First Baptist Church in East Peoria on a normal Sunday morning, Bill had overwhelmingly felt the presence of God. "The Holy Spirit came over me in a way I'd never experienced," he said. "I was so overcome with emotion, I just sat and sobbed like a baby. I clearly heard God calling me to the ministry."

After the service, Bill went to the pastor's office for advice on how to deal with God's call on his life. The pastor counseled him, "It was just an emotional experience. God doesn't really speak to people like that today. Just keep on with your Sunday School teaching and directing our youth ministries. You need to let it cool down for a while."

Bill heeded his pastor's advice, and "let it cool down," though he was still convinced God wanted him in full-time ministry some day. The first year or so of our marriage were rough on Bill. He was attending college, working part-time at a car dealership, and building our house. Then I had emergency surgery in the first trimester of pregnancy, and most the housekeeping chores fell on him as well. Occasionally, the doctor's warning flashed across my mind, and I would caution Bill to slow down a little. But his health was good, and his annual checkups at the Mayo Clinic were reassurances. The Mayo doctors told him, "One day, we're going to have to repair those heart valves, but we don't want to risk it until it's absolutely necessary. Meanwhile, we'll just keep an eye on you and hope that open-heart surgery techniques continue to improve."

Heart transplants and open-heart and bypass surgeries were still in the distant future. The best we could hope for was that Bill's heart would continue to function until the medical world figured out a way to fix it.

Still mindful of God's call on our lives, we worked diligently in our local church, studying, preparing for the day Bill's health would be restored and we would go into full-time ministry. We lived in anticipation of that day when heart surgery would correct all his problems. But each year, Bill returned from his annual checkup at Mayo's with the news, "Not yet."

We built a three-bedroom house and soon filled the extra bedrooms with Billy, Jr. in 1956 and Mari in 1957. Our family complete, Bill took a nice, safe job as an engineering draftsman at Caterpillar Tractor Co., and I became a professional secretary for the same corporation. We had excellent insurance, which would certainly cover the heavy expenses of open-heart surgery. Our long-range plans called for us to keep our positions at Caterpillar, let the insurance pay for the surgery, and then serve the Lord on the rural mission field when Bill's heart was repaired.

While we were waiting, God sent us to several small churches as pulpit supply and eventually called Bill to serve as tent-making pastor to a couple of churches near our home in Central Illinois. This enabled us to fulfill our call to ministry, still protected by the security blanket of Caterpillar insurance.

Bill became increasingly restless with this plan, his burden for rural America intensifying. In the fall of 1963, on our way home from work, he surprised me by pulling into a parking lot at Detweiller Park. He shut off the engine and turned to me, a serious look on his face. "Dollie, the clock is ticking. I can't wait any longer. I want to apply to the RHMA and go full time!"

A lot of "what ifs" troubled my mind, but Bill seemed so certain, I knew God was speaking to him. "If that's what you feel God wants us to do, let's go for it," I agreed.

Others didn't see it quite the same way, trying to discourage us from "doing anything hastily." Eight years of waiting was hasty? Bill's dad, especially, was against the plan. "Are you crazy?" he demanded. "Who's going to pay for your heart surgery if you give up your job? Who's going to take care of Dollie and the kids when your heart gets worse?"

With his usual, gracious spirit, Bill tried to calm his father's fears. "Dad, I know beyond a doubt that this is God's plan for us. God will take care of everything if we just trust Him."

"And I suppose if you thought God wanted you to go out on the expressway and stand in front of an 18-wheeler barreling down on you, you'd do it?" Dad demanded.

Bill considered his dad's question. "Yes, if I was this certain that it was God's will, I'd also expect Him to protect me."

Dad finally relented and became one of our staunch supporters, although we often suspected he continued to doubt our sanity.

We went through the mission application process, were accepted by the Rural Home Missionary Association, resigned our positions at Caterpillar and in our church, and headed for the Endless Mountains of northeastern Pennsylvania. Thus began a journey of faith that took us 800 miles from home, at least 60 years back in time, and light years ahead spiritually.

While the rest of the world struggled through the turbulent '60s, we were tucked away in the remote community of Riggs in northern Appalachia, having the time of our lives.

CHAPTER 1

Expectations meet reality

I have learned, in whatsoever state I am, therewith
to be content. Philippians 4:11b

hen Rev. Longenecker suggested that Grace Baptist Church in Riggs, Pennsylvania, would be a good fit for us, I was ecstatic. I poured over pictures of quaint New England villages, gorgeous white churches with spires reaching grandly skyward, picket fences swathed in climbing roses—what an ideal place for our very first missionary assignment!

We envisioned our new field as not too much different from home. Our town resembled the pictures of New England, boasting beautiful tree-lined streets, pristine farmland, and tidy farmhouses. Settled by Mennonite farmers, Central Illinois benefited from their influence. Its well-kept farms, mint-condition machinery, and park-like lawns all spoke of the Mennonite motto: "Cleanliness is next to Godliness."

Both Bill and I had enjoyed detasseling corn every summer as teens on many of those farms. How often we had lounged in the front lawns of those farmsteads, eating our lunch and taking a break from walking the mile-long rows of corn. When the big yellow bus loaded with 30 or 40 of us teenage workers would pull up to the side yard of the farmhouse at noon, we raced for the porch swings or the

nearest shade, eager for an hour of pure bliss. Ah, yes, those Illinois farms were rural utopia!

Could Pennsylvania farms be any less? After all, the Keystone State had its share of Mennonite farmers. Isn't that where the Pennsylvania Dutch lived? We blithely made our plans to resign our executive jobs, sell our furniture and property, and head for the hills. We thought the only difference between our current home and our future ministry was that Illinois farmland was flat and Pennsylvania's farms were built in the mountains. Ignorance is bliss!

With great anticipation and even greater naiveté, we loaded the car and trailer and headed east. Bill and Mari, typical 8- and 7-year-olds, incessantly asked, "Are we there yet? How much farther is it?" Their constant barrage of questions slowed down some as we picked up Route 6 and headed across the northern tier of Pennsylvania, through the amazing Allegheny Mountains. Carved out of miles of wilderness, the scenic route had appropriately been dubbed "One of America's most beautiful drives."

To us flatlanders, it was a natural fantasyland. We gaped and stared, stopping the car every mile or so to take in yet another panoramic view of bucolic farmland, stone fences, grazing cows, winding streams, and forested hills. The kids strained to catch a glimpse of a white-tailed deer or a red fox as the road meandered between forest vistas, occasionally broken by quaint hamlets and grand, historic houses built by timber and oil barons. Our first impression of northern Pennsylvania was of serenity, tranquility, and beauty. Oh yes, we were going to love this new life of ours.

After hundreds of miles on the road, Billy and Mari grew tired of scenic gawking and began whining. "Aren't we there yet? Are we ever going to get there?"

To be honest, we weren't quite sure where "there" was. The Pennsylvania state map showed our target area, a triangle anchored by Ulster, Milan, and East Smithfield. The interior of the triangle was totally blank, showing no roads, no nothing. We also had a roughly drawn map from the folks in Riggs, telling us to take the

Ulster-East Smithfield Road out of Ulster to Riggs. Riggs itself wasn't even a hiccup on the map. As we neared Towanda, all of our adrenalin glands kicked in—we were almost there! Both kids sat on the edge of their seats, and Bill and I both sat forward as if our body motion would propel us to our new home faster.

After searching around the tiny burg of Ulster for the designated road toward East Smithfield, we finally wised up and asked a young gas station attendant for directions. "Riggs? Never heard of it," came the reply. About then, an old-timer in overalls and a squat felt hat ambled over. "You 'uns looking for Riggs? Wal, it's right up that road a piece." He proceeded to give us a tangle of directions, "mile or so past Brown's farm, turn past the next farm on yer right, then you'll hit Saco Road, veer off toward East Smithfield.... I reckon Hiram Blow's place is about the only farm left out that way."

"Tangle of roads" was an apt description of the dozens of roads that crisscrossed and meandered through what the map showed as a blank triangle. Apparently none of the roads was considered adequate to be drawn on a map, but roads there were, roads aplenty. We took the road the old-timer pointed out, whispered a prayer for guidance, and began our wanderings in the wilderness. The main difference between Moses and us at that point was that Moses had a cloud to follow. We couldn't even find a road sign to tell us where we were.

A few bad turns and many miles further, we found our destination. An old weathered church sign proclaimed "Grace Baptist Church." But where was Riggs?

We were still out in the country, miles from anything that even faintly resembled a town or an inhabited community. Next to the church was a trailer and a tiny house of sorts; across the road about half a block away was what we figured must be Hiram Blow's farm, a weathered-gray house surrounded by dilapidated outbuildings. No tree-lined streets met our gaze. No grocery store, no bank, no picket fences or pillared porches, not even a disreputable saloon. Nothing but the blacktopped road we were on and a couple of dirt roads veering off up the hill in either direction. I swallowed hard. This was the target community we hoped to reach for Christ? Where was the community?

Bewildered, we pulled up to the little gray asbestos-shingled church in the glen. Not quite the pristine New England church we had envisioned, but it did have a bell tower! Tired and run-down looking, it fairly begged us to perk it up, get some new life flowing in and out of it. Even though we were exhausted from our long journey over the mountains, the sight of our new church kick-started the adrenalin, and we wanted to begin right then, pulling weeds, planting flowers, painting, fixing. That little church would soon be humming with activity!

Our reality check hit when a door opened on the house trailer next to the church. An elderly lady poked her head out the door and said, "'Spose you're the new preacher. Wal, you'll wish you were right back in Peoria when you see that mess up there!"

She directed us to the parsonage, "up the hill apiece," sending us off with, "Don't say I didn't warn ya!"

Still optimistic, Bill and I looked at each other and shrugged, as if to say, "How bad can it be?" We had already fallen in love with our new mission field—a land of winding rivers and gurgling streams, covered bridges, mountain ranges as far as the eye could see—truly a land of unparalleled beauty. Whatever we lived in couldn't be too bad, surrounded by such magnificent proof of God's creative hand.

Or could it? As Puny tugged and towed the loaded U-Haul up the steep dirt road, we saw a large red-shingled house perched atop the hill, like a feudal castle reigning over its kingdom. The feudal part was close, at least age-wise. As we grew closer, we saw it was a circa 1700s farmhouse that had most recently been used for grain storage. No towering trees shaded it, nor were there any pretty flowerbeds or shrubs. Just a plain, tall building covered with ugly red asphalt shingles. A newer cement block building stood behind it, apparently a doorless garage. But the views of the surrounding Endless Mountains were magnificent.

When we walked around to the back, we saw that someone had been digging close to the house. Just then a pickup truck pulled into the yard, and a man who introduced himself as "one of the deacons" climbed out and strolled over to us. It seems the deep well pump had quit and the house had no water available. "Thank God you're here now," the deacon said, patting Bill on the shoulder. "Now you can figure it out!"

Our RHMA field director, Maynard Mathewson, drove up from his field at Oregon Hill to help us unload the U-Haul. As we carried our things into the dismal wreckage, I became more and more discouraged, trying hard to keep the tears in check until he left. When our new "boss" finally told us goodbye, the dam broke, and I cried. And cried. And cried. Buckets!

I should have saved those buckets of tears to use in the next few water-deprived days. For more than a week, we dragged water up the mountain in five-gallon milk cans, rationing baths in the hot, sticky weather, trying to keep the kids clean enough to impress our new parishioners. With no water supply, attempting to clean the ancient building and wash down shelves so we could unpack sorely tested our ingenuity, not to mention our patience. In its vacant days, the house had become home to hornets, wasps, and sidewinders, and looked more like an ancient dirt-floored soddy than an honest-to-goodness house.

The elderly woman, Vina Keir, had rightly warned us, we had a mess that wouldn't quit. No water, so I couldn't get cabinets clean to unpack things. I looked in vain for a place to hang all the clothes we'd brought and found nary a closet or even a clothes rod in the entire house. Adding to my frustration, everything that we packed in the previously-used missionary barrels smelled like sour milk. It all had to be washed and ironed again.

Billy's room had a bare wood floor that had never been painted, which meant we had to paint it before we could put his things in there. We just piled his bed in the living room with a mountain of other junk. In order to meet the deadline to return the U-Haul, we unloaded everything in the middle of the living room, where it sat for the next few days while we tried to get the parsonage in livable shape.

In our first letter home to my mom, I bemoaned the frustration of our first few days in the mountaintop parsonage:

> *All in all, it could be a whole lot better; on the other hand, I suppose it could be worse! Upchuck green walls, undulating linoleum floors, ochre drapes hanging like wilted zucchini. Once we get some country wallpaper in here and get some gingham curtains square dancing at the windows, it might not be too bad. I think we'll leave the rolling floors; they'll make good speed bumps for all the cockroaches.*

> *I just finished painting Billy's floor and all the doorsteps while Bill and the kids went down to Witties' for three milk cans of water, our ration for tonight and tomorrow. Someone loaned us a hot plate, on which I heated enough water to do dishes and scrub the refrigerator. Each night, Bill uses what's left of the bath water to flush the toilet. Mari and I have both had diarrhea, which doesn't help the situation any.*

> *On the brighter side, we can see three mountain ranges from our yard, and the road out here from town is one of the most scenic drives I've ever seen. It looks a lot like the Smokies, only not quite so high. Our closest neighbor came up today with some cookies; they live about three blocks down the hill and across the hayfield from here. Somewhere on the other side of us are another family and a cemetery, but we haven't seen their house yet.*

> *Our people are all real nice (at least the ones we've met already). Some of them seem to be quite embarrassed at the*

shape the parsonage is in. Once we get some water in this place, I'm sure all our troubles will be little ones. We need some screens upstairs, too; there's a lovely big room up there, but until we can open some windows it's too stuffy to use.

In a week or two when we get things all fixed up, we'll look back at all this and laugh, but right now it's kind of a mess! Last night we put our milk in the deepfreeze (it's a beaut!) to keep it cool, so this morning we had real "ice milk" for breakfast. The deepfreeze has really come in handy—we're also using it as a table until we can dig the dining room set out. Well, better go get a bath with my milk can of water. Just hope I can get all the paint off! Write to us real soon; I get homesick every once in awhile, and the kids do, too, I think.

Ah, sweet optimism! While we were back in our comfy, modern home in Illinois, we had corresponded with the folks from the church in Pennsylvania and were often amused by their letters. One letter described the "lovely wood cook stove in the parsonage kitchen," and Bill and I laughed together. "What a sense of humor these folks have!" we exclaimed, not realizing that some areas in America did indeed still use wood as cooking fuel. And that we would soon be among their number.

Another letter assured us they would "provide our heating fuel," adding that there was a large stand of trees readily available; all we had to do was go out and chop it down and stack it in the garage for our winter supply. Again, we thought they were joking and had a good laugh. Didn't every home in the United States have a gas or oil furnace, complete with a handy thermostat on the wall? However, they failed to mention that a former pastor had taken the wood-heating stove when he left, leaving us to shiver through many cold mountain nights until we could afford to buy our own wood heater.

In retrospect, I can't believe how naïve we were. Still in our mid-twenties, we suffered the normal arrogance, immaturity, and idealism of post-college youth. Two years younger than Bill, I especially had a heap of growing up to do. Pity that first congregation that had to put up with my learning curve!

The mountaintop community was not only 800 miles from our home, it was light years away in contemporary comforts. Culturally, it was like traveling back in time to the 1920s or '30s. We were appalled by the lack of modern amenities, yet thrilled by the old-fashioned values of neighborliness and friendship. People from miles around came to bring us largesse from their gardens, home-baked goodies, and cast-off furniture.

When we finally got the deep-well jet pump installed, we had water problems of a different nature. Every pipe in the house leaked, thanks to dried gaskets from lack of use. It was drip drip, here, drip, drip there, drip, drip everywhere! But the big bathroom with its broken claw-foot bathtub held up on a couple of bricks looked mighty fine when we discovered we had the only bathroom in our immediate neighborhood. A little fellow from church was visiting one day and beheld the wonders of our modern bathtub for the first time. "Wow!" he exclaimed. "Look at that big sink!"

Despite the lack of modern conveniences, some of our church folks managed to have lovely outhouse facilities. It seemed they tried to outdo each other in outhouse decorating, some having wallpaper and curtains; one family even had a scrap of plush carpeting on the floor of their three-holer.

Our goal in going to the mountains was to preach the Gospel, not to raise their standard of living or change their cultural ideas. We decided it would be *our* cultural ideas that would get changed. Like Paul, we would become all things to all people, adapting ourselves to a new way of life, that we "might by any means save some."

If that meant learning to cook on a wood stove, using an outhouse down the "path" instead of our accustomed "bath," chopping wood, mucking out barns, maple sugaring, putting in hay, dining in church members' homes while chickens free-ranged all over the kitchen and fly paper dangled above the table, so be it. With God's help we could do it.

Wit-n-wisdom: The will of God will never lead us where the sufficiency of God's grace can't keep us.

CHAPTER 2

Adapting to Country Life

He whose throne is in heaven sits laughing—
Psalm 2:4 (Author's free translation)

When we made the move from corporate employees in Illinois to country parson in rural Pennsylvania, we had to change a lot more than our wardrobe. Actually, I was enthused about the move. "Country Living Magazine" wouldn't hit the newsstands for another decade and "country style" had yet to enter the interior designer's vocabulary, but I was years ahead of the decorating trend. Baskets dangled from every available beam, and ducks and geese quacked their way across our walls and all my tea towels. I was a country girl at heart.

Neither Bill nor I thought we'd have any trouble fitting into the country culture. Even though we'd lived a relative life of ease in lower Suburbia, we had grown up in a rural area. Sort of.

Bill's family had about an acre plot two or three miles from town and always planted large gardens. My dad had ten acres just down the road from the Farleys, and back then, ten acres was a real farm. All our neighbors were truck farmers, carting their raspberries, apples, cider, and veggies off to the local market every week in their farm trucks. And we all had a couple of cows and one or two sows on our "farms."

So I was no stranger to watering cows and slopping hogs, and Bill had done his share of hoeing and weeding. It's true neither of us had ever milked a cow, but at least we knew you didn't pump the tail to get milk.

But in Pennsylvania, those farmers talked a whole new lingo. On one of our first ventures into the hinterlands to visit a church member, Stub Wittie, one of the deacons, gave us directions. "Go down the dirt road for a couple of miles, then turn left on the McAdam Highway." We drove for hours on the dirt road, back and forth, trying to find a road marked "McAdam Highway." Finally, we gave up our quest and asked a nearby farmer where that highway was. He pointed to a blacktop road just ahead. "Wal, it's right there," he said. How were we to know that in the local vernacular "macadam" meant blacktop?

About that same time we also figured out that "the berm" was the side of the road, what we called a shoulder. Stranger yet was the local euphemism the kids used when they asked to be excused to "go to the basement." What could they possibly want to do down in that dark, dirty cellar? For some unknown reason, "going to the basement" was synonymous with "going to the bathroom." As far as we knew, none of them had ever seen a bathroom in a basement— most of them didn't even have bathrooms inside. Who knows the origins of that particular phrase???

When one of our new parishioners, a widow lady, got in trouble with the milk inspectors, Bill gallantly offered to help. After all, he often cut Billy's hair, so what could be difficult about clipping cows? How was a well-trained engineer to know that clipping cows meant crawling around underneath the beautiful bovines, shearing off hair matted with animal droppings? To Bill's credit, he performed the dirty duty without complaining, winning the admiration and respect of many a born and bred dairyman.

While Bill was up at the dairy barn doing his thing, the ladies in the farmhouse down the mountain were entertaining me. Suddenly the phone rang and a loud voice shouted a nerve-shattering message. "Come quick! Billy just fell in the drop!"

I immediately imagined my little boy bruised and battered and broken, maybe a concussion or a skull fracture, even. What was a "drop?" How far did he fall? Those questions raced through my mind, but I didn't stop to ask. I ran up the mountain to rescue my injured son, ready to call the medics, an ambulance, or the coroner.

As I entered the barn, sounds of raucous laughter shook the rafters. There stood the men, gingerly yanking Billy from the yucky "drop," the shallow trench behind the cow stanchions, where the cows just naturally "drop" their "droppings."

Had Billy been covered with blood, I would have rushed to his side and folded him to my motherly breast. As it was, I wouldn't get near him with a ten-foot pole. I lined the back seat of the car with newspaper, ordered him not to touch a thing, and sped toward home. Despite Lysol, Pinesol, and Hexol, our house smelled like a dairy barn for weeks.

It wasn't the first time the local farmers had a good laugh at the expense of us city slickers. The first day we landed at the mountaintop parsonage, Stub eagerly took us around back to show off the garden he had lovingly started for us, but which had since grown up in weeds.

Determined to get my country act together and prove I was worthy of my calling, I tackled those weeds with all the gusto of Willie Nelson saving the Iowa farms. When Stub returned a few days later, I proudly took him around back to the garden to show off my efforts.

I wasn't prepared for the laughing fit he had—weren't New England farmers supposed to stand around holding pitchforks and Nonconformist hymnbooks, somber frowns on their faces, the way Norman Rockwell painted 'em?

Instead, Stub virtually rolled in the rows, laughing hysterically. When he finally quit sputtering enough to be understood, he said,

13

"You sure did a great job. You pulled up all the Swiss chard and left a nice row of ragweed in its place!"

Swiss chard? I thought that was a cheese, sort of a cross between the holey stuff and cheddar. My gardening efforts that year nearly qualified me for government disaster payments. The woodchucks ate the peas, the deer got the corn, and there were so many snakes in the bean patch, I was scared to go in for the harvest.

My garden wasn't a total disaster, however. My potato crop turned out great. Some of those spuds were as big as golf balls, some were the size of marbles, and some looked like brown peas. Then, of course, there were a few little ones.

The neighborly mountain folk more than made up for my gardening ineptness, generously sharing the fruits of their labors with us. Summer squash, zucchini, tomatoes—anything they had grown in abundance found its way into my kitchen. They often invited us to help ourselves in their gardens, a fact which immensely helped our grocery bill. One evening we went down to the Witties' bean patch, a field right on the creek bank. The weeds were about knee-high so it was hard to find the vegetables. Just as I pulled back some weeds to reach the bean plant, a snake wiggled up the row in front of me. Bill and Billy finally got him and threw him on the other side of the creek, but it took me much longer to calm down. It was with trembling hand and pounding heart that I finally bent over and started searching through the weeds for the beans. My courage paid off; the next day I managed to get 18 big sacks of green beans in the freezer, a rash on my arms and legs, and an aching back to show for my efforts.

Stub also introduced us to the wonders of berry picking. Huckleberries, choke cherries, raspberries, blackberries, serviceberries—they were all ours for the picking. He made certain we were aware of the rules for berry picking, unwritten rules that generations of berry pickers had formulated and everyone must know before trekking out to the bushes. Rule number 1: "Thou shalt not pick from a bush another hath located first." In other words, Stub said, "Find your own bush and leave mine alone."

Each of us ambled off to the huckleberry patch, diligently finding our own choice spot to harvest. Soon we heard Stub bellow, "Get out of here! This bush is mine!" Amidst the rattle and rustle of berry leaves, the offender hulked around to Stub's side of the bush. Growling and pawing the bushes, an enormous black bear let us know in no uncertain terms who had first right of ownership to the berry patch. We all grabbed our pails and ran, all too eager to "get out of here!"

For an ex-career gal who had spent precious little time in a kitchen, trying to cook and preserve all those bonus beauties brought many surprises and more than a few "crop failures." However, I was doing passably well in my new profession as country parson's wife, at least until the grapes began to ripen.

The first few neighbors who arrived at the parsonage door with buckets full of purple grapes were warmly received. Fresh grapes, fresh squeezed grape juice—yum! But when the whole family came down with a severe case of the proverbial willy-wobbles, BYTs, or whatever else you call them, I decided it was time to preserve some of those grapes for later enjoyment.

Blowing the dust off my Betty Crocker Cookbook (an as-yet unused wedding gift from my optimistic mother-in-law), I found a recipe for making grape jelly and set to work. Hours later, with purple countertops, purple fingers, purple floors and purple clothes, I fell into bed exhausted. My last coherent words were, "If I ever see another grape, I'll scream!"

Early the next morning, we were awakened by a knock at the door. There stood Hiram Blow, a huge bucket of grapes in each hand. I pasted on my best parsonage smile and graciously accepted the gift, holding back the scream until Hiram was well out of earshot.

Bill quickly came to my rescue with his never-fail advice. "Call Mom. She'll know what to do with all those grapes." She did. A no-fail recipe for grape juice. All I had to do was pour boiling water over a cup of grapes in each jar, dump in some sugar, and the job was done. Even a dingbat housewife like me could handle that.

Jars of sparkling grape juice soon adorned my shelves, and my hard-to-convince husband finally admitted I might make it in the culinary department. He begged to taste my fruit of the vine, but I persuaded him to wait.

Our boss at the RHMA, the eminent Doctor-Reverend Harold Longenecker, planned to visit in a couple of months. That would be soon enough to break out my achievements and justify his faith in our abilities to serve a country church.

When the Big Day arrived, I had the parsonage spit and polished, set out my best china, and dolled the kids up to look like normal preacher's kids instead of the country ragamuffins they usually were. For the coup de gracé, I poured sparkling grape juice into crystal goblets.

Just as I caught a glimpse of Harold's car cruising up our mountain, I heard Bill gasping and choking in the dining room. "This stuff's turned into wine," he gasped, holding out the goblet he had snitched a sip from. "Didn't you seal those bottles?"

Seal the bottles? His mother hadn't said anything about sealing bottles. Leaving the boss knocking at the front door, we rushed out the back, trying to dispose of the incriminating evidence. As we poured the sparkling red liquid down the rear gully, Harold decided to try the back door. He caught us, literally red handed.

Old blabbermouth Bill couldn't resist telling the whole story, embellishing it a bit. Speaking of my efforts to make jelly and juice, he said, "Dollie's been a real angel about all this farm life—always up in the air harping about something!"

Good-natured fellow that he is, Harold replied, "Well, Christ turned water into wine. Surely it's all right for an angel to turn grape juice into wine." He said his only regret was that he hadn't arrived early enough for the tasting party.

Wit-n-wisdom: Happy are they who laugh at their own mistakes, for they shall lead joyful lives!

CHAPTER 3

Full Steam Ahead

*...he which converteth the sinner from the error of his way shall save a
soul from death, and shall hide a multitude of sins—James 5:20*

*J*ust as we had tackled the gardening and farming chores
with such gusto, our enthusiasm for the ministry held
equal fervor and passion ... possibly more passion than
common sense. We had arrived in Riggs on Wednesday, right after
the Fourth of July holiday. Four days later, Bill was already in the
pulpit, preaching his first sermon to our new congregation.

We described that first service in a letter to our folks:

> *Attendance was 21 yesterday ... the weather was so
> miserable most of the farmers just didn't move fast enough
> to get their chores done on time. It was quite a service,
> with babies bawling and fussy, flies crawling all over Bill
> as he tried to preach, and wasps flirting around every once
> in awhile.*
>
> *There were eight senior high girls in church, and Bill could
> barely be heard over their racket. Laughing, giggling, and
> talking loudly during the entire service, apparently they
> had never been taught that silence in church is a virtue.*

Needless to say, it affected Bill's message, too, and he was kind of discouraged about the whole thing. Last night more than made up for it, though. It cooled off a little and 34 showed up, and the Holy Spirit could just be felt all over the church, especially in the sermon. You could just tell He had control of Bill. Some of our young people who left to go to other churches were back, one of them with his trumpet. He played for the congregational singing, then he and I played a special. For being completely unrehearsed and the piano out of tune, it didn't sound too bad. I felt sorry for him at first, when he was trying to find out what key I was playing in, until he finally discovered the piano was terribly out of tune.

* * *

Apparently the piano hadn't been played in a very long time. That first Sunday they told me they needed a piano player badly. My three sisters were all talented musicians, but the ability-to-play-by-ear gene passed me by, and I struggled to learn music. From the time I was a little girl, I wanted to play the piano in the worst way. So Grace Baptist Church and I made a good match. They got a bad piano player, and I played in the worst way.

As is customary for most rural preacher's wives, I was immediately assigned a seat on the piano bench, given directorship of the Sunday School and youth groups, voted president of the Ladies' Missionary Group and the Good Neighbor Club, "volunteered" to teach several weekly Good News Clubs, plus expected to go calling frequently with the pastor. We were so young and naïve back then, we didn't realize the word "no" was in our vocabulary.

Less than two weeks into our ministry, we gathered up 25 young people and took them over the mountain to Troy to see the Christian film, "Lucia. " It had a wonderful evangelistic message, and as eight young people went forward to accept Christ, I was praying fervently for our own teens. I turned around to check on them, only to discover they had skipped out during intermission and didn't bother to come back. How our hearts ached for those kids! Most of them were from broken or dysfunctional homes, and we determined with God's help to love them into the Kingdom.

Puny described our trip to see "Lucia" in his August prayer letter, complaining about the mountain roads:

These crazy, rollercoaster mountain roads! They'd tax the ingenuity of a Jeep, let alone a little city-born car like me! I've been real good about getting Mr. Farley around on his calls, but one night when the Missus ventured out alone, she really got me confused. She still thinks the sun rises and sets on the wrong side of the mountain.

Anyway, we took a bunch over to Troy to see a Billy Graham movie the other night. When taking the teenagers home afterwards, we wound around and around, up hill and down, and my gas gauge slipped closer and closer to EMPTY. Now, if you know anything at all about these mountain back roads, you know gas stations are hard enough to find in the day time, let alone at midnight. I was doing my best to conserve gas, but those dirt roads make me awfully thirsty. And, as much as I hate to say so, I'll admit I'm something of a gas addict, so I was just a little worried about getting them home myself. Just as my carburetor coughed up its last few dredges of the delicious stuff, we met another carload of our group coming the other way (on these one-lane roads you don't "pass" another car, you "meet" it—hood to hood.) They told me to back down the hill to their farm (quite a feat in itself!!), where they gave me enough gas to wind around on home.

There's been some mighty strange things going on lately ... early one morning someone sneaked up the drive and put a jar of milk on my hood! One night after church, somebody

21

opened my back door and quietly stuck a big sack of potatoes on my seat. I don't understand what's happening, but the Farleys certainly seem to appreciate it. These folks sure take good care of my owners.

Shortly after our excursion to Troy, again with more zeal than sense, we decided to have a Vacation Bible School. Our old-timers tried to squelch the idea, telling us no one would come, no one would help, and it would be a waste of time and money. We solved the money part by scrounging through the boxes of stuff stored away in the church and parsonage, items that apparently hadn't seen the light of day in years. We found two full boxes of supplies, with enough scissors, crayons, stickers, pencils, etc., to start our own store. The Lord sent us two Child Evangelism Fellowship summer missionaries to help out, and we were off and running.

We had 63 kids out the first day, which tied the church's all-time record VBS attendance. The big turnout thrilled our hearts, especially since the people were so pessimistic about having a VBS that year. It was cold and rainy (a high of 70 degrees on Aug. 3?? That's mountain weather for you!), so we had all those yelling, rowdy kids inside, even for recess. We really beat the bushes to find the kids—we had no idea what would be involved with picking kids up all around the mountain, over muddy, nearly impassable roads for miles and miles.

There were several "pockets" of kids we didn't even try to reach, because we didn't have enough cars available to pick them up. We arranged for the CEF missionaries to set up clubs in those neighborhoods, so the children would get to hear the same lessons.

We continued to break all attendance records that week, with a total enrollment of 74. More than 100 came to the picnic Friday afternoon, and the best count we could get at the closing program was 90. That poor little church was really straining at the seams. Best of all was the shouting up in Heaven over the five kids who asked Jesus to come into their lives.

I doubt if the CEF girls will ever forget their time in the Endless Mountains. We had some real characters in our congregation, fun-loving, goofy practical jokers. The Wilcox family hosted the missionaries during VBS, and every day the girls had a wild story to relate. The first night they came home late and found a "man" in their bed. The next day when Dora opened the bathroom door, the same "man" was sitting on the john. We happened to be out at the Wilcoxes' doing our laundry when Dora encountered him, and her face said it all ... utter shock, horror, and disbelief. She gasped and slammed the door, then motioned for me to look. I knew about the dummy, having been a victim of the same joke a week earlier, but it was so real, it even startled me.

George Wilcox had rigged up all kinds of booby traps, a short-sheeted bed, rubber snakes and spiders in the bed, loosened saltshaker lids. But he didn't stop at standard camp tricks. His pranks were much more ingenious than that. He plied the girls with tales of a ghost who haunted the old farmhouse and almost had us all believing the place was haunted. One night as the girls were sleeping, their sheets began slipping away and something kept pushing the bed up. They were certain someone was under the bed but couldn't find anything amiss. George and Mary had rigged a pulley in their room next door and were manipulating the girls' bed from their side of the wall ... the ghost of Wilcox Valley.

Because we had no washing machine, I often did our laundry at the Wilcox farm, and more than once I was surprised by a squiggly, wriggly black rubber spider in a pocket, so we should have expected our guests would get the same treatment. We knew missionary work would be fruitful, but in our wildest imaginations, we hadn't dreamed it would be so much fun!

We attended three weddings just a week or so after we arrived on the field. George and Mary Wilcox were married one day, the next day George Blow took a bride. The second George borrowed the first George's wedding sportscoat to wear at his own wedding. That's real Endless Mountain neighborliness for you!

Soon after the weddings, we were introduced to a crazy custom we had only heard about in the history books. About 10 o'clock one night, cars silently pulled into a barnyard near the newlyweds' house, doused their lights, and all their occupants crept out. The "horning" was on. Our plan was to visit both newlywed couples that night. The custom was to sneak outside their window after they've gone to bed. Then a telltale shotgun blast wakes them up, and all sorts of orneriness breaks loose. The participants stand outside making as much noise as possible until the newlyweds finally get up and invite the group in for refreshments.

Trying to keep everyone quiet until the gun went off at both houses provided more excitement than we'd ever had in the city. I fell into a rose bush and couldn't help yelling "Ouch!" to a chorus of "Shhhhh!" What a motley crew we were, trudging up the mountain road, with a weird assortment of washtubs, buzz saws, shotguns, cow horns, cowbells, and whatever other noisemakers we could find. One car passed us very slowly, and we could just imagine them saying, "What are those crazy Baptists up to now?"

The first couple we "hit" was totally surprised and didn't have anything to offer the celebrants except a box of sour cherries. We all ate them, then when the newlyweds' backs were turned, someone gathered up the pits and scattered them in the bridal bed.

George and Mary Wilcox were staying at his family farm, where his sister Esther was visiting that week. By mistake, we went to her window and woke up her five kids. His mother, our accomplice, had fixed a lot of refreshments for the occasion. Among the goodies was a spice cake without frosting. Esther demanded icing on her cake, so George piled a square of the cake high with mayonnaise and presented it to her with great flourish. She took a big bite of it, spit and sputtered, then chased him around the farmhouse, smearing it all over his face. I think that's when we first began to fall in love with these fun-loving people. Someone had an accordion and a guitar handy, so we all sat around singing and laughing till 1 a.m.

We got our own "horning" just a month later for our wedding anniversary on September 2. Fortunately for us, the parsonage's location on top the hill usually provided fair warning when someone was approaching. As soon as we heard a car groaning up the hill, we could quickly prepare for unexpected guests. That night, Bill noticed some cars down the hill and up by the cemetery, but he just thought they were coon hunters. Soon we heard crowds come sneaking up our drive, horns ablowin', guns blasting, and pots and pans pounding. The congregation caught us totally by surprise, as just a couple of hours earlier we had seen them at prayer meeting.

We weren't prepared food wise and had almost nothing in the house. They apparently had anticipated that, because they brought sandwiches, Jell-O, cake, and Kool-Aid, and had even brought their own dishes so they wouldn't leave a mess for me to clean up.

They weren't done welcoming us yet, however. The very next week, they gave us a "pounding party," where everyone for miles around came and brought a pound of food … home canned goods, staples like sugar and flour, cans of vegetables. They brought so much food, Bill told them it was more like a "tonning" party than a "pounding."

True to their fun-loving nature, many of the folks tore the labels off all the canned goods, so for weeks we ate mystery dinners. Shaking a can, thumping it, or trying to hold it up to a bright light, attempting to figure out if it contained canned corn or dog food became the regular meal routine. It also produced some mighty strange menu combinations. We were especially leery of anything that looked like hash, a great look-alike for dog food.

The dog food was for our new puppy, George, a gift from the Wilcox family and appropriately named for his donor. A tribute to our naiveté, George the puppy once again showed our absolute ignorance of animals. If anything proved we were city slickers it was our gullibility in taking a puppy with its eyes still closed and then thinking it was blind! Chalk up another big laugh at our expense! Our ability to laugh at ourselves, along with our congregation, apparently endeared us to them, removing our "outsider" status quickly.

Our social life was a big part of the ministry. Birthdays, anniversaries, anything was an excuse for a party. Following the weekly prayer meeting shortly after VBS, we all went over to surprise one of our ladies for her birthday. Someone baked Marian a cake and I made Jell-O, then about 14 of us walked up the hill to the Wittie farm to celebrate with her. Three days later, they all got together at our house for a wiener roast. The fellowship was sweet and helped us adjust quickly to our new life in the mountains—we didn't have time to get homesick.

Late night visitors became quite common after that. Dick, who worked just across the border in New York, often woke us up after his late shift, bringing us hot dogs from the city. Pennsylvania had a law against selling colored hot dogs, so whenever Dick got a hankering for a real hot dog, he'd stop at the drive-in on his way home from work and bring a sack of hot dogs for us to enjoy with him.

George and Mary Wilcox were late-nighters, too, and occasionally drove over around midnight with some harebrained, but fun, idea. Once when both Mary and I were suffering the pangs of pregnancy, she had a midnight craving for chocolate ice cream. They came and got us out of bed, then we drove for several hours trying to find a place to get our ice cream. We finally found a store open down in Wyalusing, some 50-mountain miles from home.

We were fast learning that serving as pastor to "those crazy Baptists" was an exhilarating experience, sometimes hair-raising, sometimes exhausting, but never boring.

Wit-n-wisdom: Joy is the by-product of obedience to God's will.

CHAPTER 4

Ulcers and Other Surprises

Faithful is he that calleth you, who also will do it. I Thessalonians 5:24

W e had been on our new mission field about two months and had more or less settled into life as a country parson's family. We enrolled Billy and Mari in the third and second grades, respectively, at East Smithfield Elementary School and eagerly waited for the day after Labor Day so they could begin their new adventures.

Both of them had taken to country life like bees to honey, enjoying the wide open spaces, the many trips to the woods for the never-ending wood bees, accompanying their dad when he helped our neighbors take in their hay, and even riding cows. They especially were delighted with a little orphan fawn we adopted for awhile.

Because of our position as the new parson and his family, we were readily accepted just about everywhere, giving the kids a number of new friends and playmates. Also by virtue of my position as the preacher's wife, I automatically became the church babysitter. "After all, you're home all day anyway, so I'll just drop my young'uns off for ya to keep an eye on …."

It wasn't unusual for us to have a handful of extra children hanging around while their mothers worked, either in town or in the fields with their husbands. Rarely a day passed that I didn't have at least one extra little urchin to tend. Which probably explains why I was so eager for that big yellow school bus to begin huffing up our hill!

The Friday morning before school was to start, I detailed my busy schedule in a letter to Mom:

> *Hi! Maybe someday I'll get this finished. Have last night's dishes in the sink, a crisper full of corn to freeze, bugs all over the floor to be swept up, and half a basket of ironing to do, besides going to put the notice in the Towanda paper and visiting Mildred at the hospital in Sayre. We were out of hot water again last night, so I couldn't wash the dishes—have quite a stack because Burlingames were here for supper.*
>
> *Maybe next week I'll have myself more in order, but don't count on it. Tomorrow night, we have a YBC (equivalent of Youth for Christ) Western Party, and Monday is our Sunday School picnic. I'm also trying to get the Crow's Nest painted and fixed up before the pounding party they're having here next Friday. The couple who were going to be YBC sponsors for the area had to back out, so it looks like we'll wind up with that job. I'm also supposed to teach some Bible clubs in the county schools this year, as soon as we find out what schools are still open and which ones will allow the kids released time to go somewhere nearby for their clubs.*
>
> *They've asked me to take a Girl Scout troop up at school this year. I'm going to a Council meeting tomorrow night to see what it's all about. I'm kind of undecided—it might be a real good chance to witness and reach the kids; it might also take a lot of time that could be spent more profitably elsewhere.*

* * *

Like I said, the word "no" wasn't in our vocabulary, and I added Girl Scout leader to my list of titles.

Instead of county-owned school buses, private owners bid for the school bus routes. We considered it a blessing from God that Billy and Mari would be picked up every day for school by Stub, our good friend and deacon. Stub had owned the bus route for many years and was a favorite with all the kids, ours included. Knowing a friendly bus driver would pick them up every school day relieved our minds considerably and freed me to get on with "ministry."

Like many young pastors, we made the mistake of being so busy about our Father's business, we didn't realize our first priority was the children He had entrusted to us. It wasn't until many, many years later that I learned how dreadful that daily bus ride was for Mari and Billy. It seems as the new kids and the pastor's kids to boot, they were the targets of all the high school bullies on the daily bus ride. Billy was the primary target. The older boys delighted in taunting him and giving him painful "Dutch" rubs on his crew cut head. Even though they left Mari alone for the most part, she hated seeing her big brother trying to bravely hold back the tears. On occasion, Mari would plead, "Mom, can't you drive us to school today?" But I was so busy I didn't take time to investigate why she was so eager not to ride the bus.

When, from the "safety" of adulthood, they mentioned it in conversation, I was shocked. "How can that be? Why didn't you tell us?" It seems Stub was so busy trying to drive the bus over the treacherous roads, he didn't see what was going on behind him in the bus, or I'm sure he would have mentioned it to us.

"We didn't tell you because you were so busy, and we didn't want to cause you and Daddy any trouble with the church people," they told me. The teasing and bullying did no lasting harm, and both grew up to be marvelous servants of God. But as a mother, my heart aches that my children were hurting, and I was too busy to notice.

With such busy schedules, the days sped by. Cold fall days arrived early in September, with brisk, clear days and gorgeous red sunsets. The Chamber of Commerce called it "Flaming Foliage Time in the Endless Mountains," an apt description of the spectacular tree colors. The view from our Crow's Nest office that we built in the attic was awe-inspiring, with golden fields surrounded by crimson woodlands in our near view, and range after range of flaming forest-covered mountains in the distance.

We were all fascinated by the herds of deer that roamed our mountaintop, but we were extra cautious of the bucks that all too often leaped across the road in front of our car. The farmers worked frantically to get their silage in before it spoiled, haying was critical, and we were thankful we had worked so hard to get our wood supply in before everyone got so busy on their farms.

Ever since we had arrived in July, the mountaintop parsonage was cold every morning, with summer temperatures dropping down into the 40s. The only heat in the house came from the wood cook stove in the kitchen and a small kerosene heater someone loaned us. We shivered daily in the drafty, huge house, huddling close to whatever heat we could find. Mom sent us an electric blanket, and my sister sent us a second one. Bill would huddle in bed with Billy under one blanket, while I tried to keep Mari warm in her room with the other one.

Chimney burnouts were a big threat in the mountain homes. Frequently as we drove through the country, we'd see a chimney or house foundation standing alone, grim reminders of a chimney fire that flamed out of control. One night, our house was so smoky, we had difficulty sleeping, even with the windows open and the cold wind blowing in. The next morning we were greeted with a horrible sooty mess in the kitchen—the stopper had blown out during the night during a chimney fire. We had a praise session right there on the cold kitchen floor, thanking God He had kept the sparks from setting fire to the roof.

Sometimes the fires burned so hot, the inside chimney got nearly white with heat, and we could see the flames shooting up through it. We practiced fire drills with the kids and taught them the best ways to get out, what to do, and what not to do. The stove was directly beneath the stairwell, so in case of fire, Bill and I would have to go down from our bedroom via the roof, then go outside to rescue Bill and Mari from their rooms on opposite sides of the house ... a scary proposition.

We eventually learned to live with the nuances and dangers of wood heat. When the church helped us install a wood heater in the living room, we grew accustomed to the occasional smoke and burning eyes. We loved the smell of the wood fire but hated the mess and work of the constant wood-hauling chores. What we thought would be our winter's wood supply quickly dwindled, and by mid-September we were back out in the woods again.

When my health took a nosedive, we assumed it was from the wood heat or possibly the strenuous schedule we kept. The local doctor checked me over and gave me the typical remedy for any unknown ailment, "Go home and try to get some rest." Rest was impossible at our house, so I continued all my activities, stopping only long enough to rush to the bathroom to upchuck or choke down a saltine cracker.

After several weeks of this routine, Bill insisted I go to another doctor. This one had the diagnosis. I was obviously suffering from an ulcer. She gave me ulcer medicines, told me to get some rest, and wished me well. Then the women at Ladies Missionary Society told me, "Oh, she tells everybody who goes to her with a stomach ache they have an ulcer! She told Betty she had ulcers and it turned out to be spastic colitis." Somebody else assured me her ulcer turned out to be gallstones. With such Job's comforters, I began to wonder if Vina might have been right when she loudly declared at our first ladies' meeting: "Won't be long till you get pregnant. Every preacher's wife who comes here gets pregnant right off the bat."

Shocked by her brashness, I was confident it wouldn't happen to me. We had decided to stop our family with the two God had already given us, and with Mari approaching age 8, I wasn't about to start the baby scene all over again.

Late in September, the Farleys brought my mother out from Illinois for a visit, along with storm windows and doors, a chain saw, blankets, and all sorts of items to warm up our place for the oncoming winter months. We enjoyed many visitors that month, including Rev. Longenecker, several visiting speakers, and Bill's brother and his wife. But I was almost too sick to enjoy the sightseeing and fellowship. One night during Rev. Longenecker's visit, my dry heaves were so bad, Bill rushed me up to the hospital in Sayre for a nausea shot.

At the hospital, we got an accurate diagnosis. Turned out Vina's uncanny prediction was right. With great glee, Bill told everyone the news. "Come next spring, we'll be able to spank our little ulcer for all the trouble he's caused!" I found myself thrilled at the news, as well. At least I knew there would eventually be an end to my heaving!

The next morning, because I was still very sick, Bill and Rev. Longenecker decided to fix their own breakfast. I heard them out in the kitchen laughing and joking and good naturedly arguing over which one of them had to try the first piece of French toast they had concocted.

I was so sick during the entire pregnancy, I continued to lose weight instead of gaining it. More and more, I looked like a long, skinny thermometer with its bulb in the middle. Our people became accustomed to my frequent runs to the outhouse when we were their guests. They all kept a supply of soda crackers and 7-Up on hand and kept me supplied with mints.

God continued to give me strength, despite the nausea. Some days I threw up all the way to Bible club and all the way back, but the Lord always gave me strength for that one hour of standing up in front of the kids. I kept all the Bible clubs going, kept up with the Girl Scouts, the youth group, the Sunday School, YBC, plus frequently going calling with Bill.

The winding roads were a nightmare for someone already so nauseated, so I learned to keep a barf bag in the front seat, along with the ever-present soda crackers. Somehow, no matter how sick

I happened to be, God came through and helped me with whatever assignment He had given me for the day. But God didn't just "get us through" each assignment, He abundantly blessed, and we were able to introduce many boys and girls to the Lord Jesus.

Feeling especially rotten one Friday afternoon, I almost decided not to accompany Bill to the hospital in Sayre to visit a lady who was dying of cancer. Florence's kids were involved in our youth ministry and Sunday School, but she and her husband didn't know the Lord. We had visited her many times, always received a warm welcome, and were allowed to pray with her. However, she refused to accept the Lord, just feeling no need for it.

On this particular day, the family called and said they'd taken Florence back to the hospital and that she probably would never get to come home. We prayed, then immediately went up the valley to see her. As soon as we got there, she told us she was ready to accept Christ and trust Him as her Savior. There's nothing like leading a soul to Christ to cure morning sickness!

Florence passed into eternity Sunday night, and Bill immediately went to be with the family. He didn't come home until after midnight, but when he arrived, he had a big smile on his face. "I just led Sam to the Lord!" After doing what he could for the bereaved family, Bill had stopped by to pray with Florence's parents, who lived with another daughter and her family. Sam, Florence's brother-in-law, was there, babysitting all the kids. He and his wife had visited our church that morning, when Bill preached on Romans 8:28 in relation to Florence. They left immediately after church, and Bill was afraid he had offended them by such a personal message.

Quite the contrary—Sam told him they just about came forward at the invitation that morning, but something held them back. So there he sat, all prepared and ready, and Bill just had to glean the "harvest." His wife said she had been saved and baptized as a young girl, but she wanted to rededicate her life to the Lord. Then the parents came in, and Florence's mother said, she too, had accepted

Christ in her youth but needed reassurance that she truly was a child of God.

They were all members of a liberal church in the valley, so we assumed their pastor would deliver the funeral message. But Monday morning, we received a call, asking Bill to preach it. "Nobody but Rev. Farley is going to preach my wife's funeral!" Florence's husband insisted. He was always open and friendly when we called on his wife at the hospital, but he had shown no interest in the Gospel. That evening we took some food down to the house, and the kids said their dad was milking but wanted to see Bill for "a minute."

The "minute" lasted for nearly an hour while the recent widower talked and talked. He said he'd never thought about religion before, but he definitely wanted Bill to come back in a few days after the funeral to explain it to him.

Shortly after, the entire family joined the church and became active for the Lord. We often wondered, "What if we hadn't gone to Pennsylvania? What if there had been no missionary to lead Florence and her family to the Lord?"

Wit-n-Wisdom: God's timing is always perfect. Better do it now; there may not be a tomorrow.

CHAPTER 5

Financial Woes vs. Living by Faith

My God shall supply all your need according to his riches
in glory by Christ Jesus. Philippians 4:19

hen we applied to the RHMA to become rural missionaries, we knew it was a faith mission. Missionaries received no salaries but did something called "deputation," inviting friends, relatives, and churches to share financially in their ministry. This is a tried-and-true method of supporting God's work, one that has been in existence since St. Paul thanked the Philippian church for its generosity while he was in Thessalonica.

Before going to Pennsylvania, we shared our burden for the folks in the Endless Mountains with several churches in our home area and discussed it with fellow workers at Caterpillar in our after-hours Bible studies. It was a simple plan. Friends promised to partner with us by praying for us and sending their financial gifts to the RHMA office, where staff designated the gift to our account and sent the donor a receipt for tax purposes. Once a month, the RHMA sent us whatever had accumulated in our account for that month.

We had absolutely no trouble believing that God would supply all our needs. Hadn't He taken marvelous care of us in the past? We had good salaries, regular paychecks, and few money worries.

True, we had gone through some difficult times when Bill was laid off from Caterpillar during the recession, but even then, God had provided. Back in the late 50s, when life looked the bleakest because no jobs were available, God gave Bill an engineering job at the Harley-Davidson Motorcycle Company in Milwaukee. The move to Milwaukee totally changed the direction of our lives. Our home church was a very liberal one, and all of our youth ministries had been through the area Council of Churches, the state denomination, and other entities on the liberal side of theology. Though we were busy in the church all our lives, we knew very little about the Bible, the Lord, or winning the lost for Jesus.

Our financial situation at the time precluded any extra money for gas, so we checked the telephone book to locate a Baptist church close to our apartment. The Lord led us to a little Baptist church in the early stages of development, planted by Rev. Grant Rice. He became our spiritual mentor, Bible teacher, and encourager. Under his tutelage, we hungrily soaked in Bible truths, began hosting Child Evangelism Clubs, and became youth leaders with an entirely new mission—a desire to win kids for Christ!

During those days we learned to totally lean upon the Lord for our daily bread. Grant Rice taught us to pray about our needs and expect God to answer. One evening Grant taught us, "There is nothing too small for God to answer. Take all your needs to Him."

When he left the house that night, Bill hurried out to the store to buy a few groceries. Knowing the state of our budget, and also knowing Bill's penchant for loading up a grocery cart with "extras," I playfully admonished him, "Don't you dare buy a thing that isn't on that list!"

Right after he left, I realized we didn't have a bit of butter or oil in the house, so how could I fix the pancakes or eggs I had planned for breakfast? God reminded me about that night's lesson: *Pray about everything. Nothing is too small to pray about.* Anything, Lord?

Bill came home a few minutes later and put the grocery bag on the kitchen counter. Smiling, he held up a pound of butter. "You prayed about this, didn't you?"

I nodded. "I stuck to your list exactly," he said. "But just as I rounded the aisle to head for the check-out, a lady bumped her cart into mine and a pound of butter bounced out. I bent over to pick it up for her and remembered we needed butter for the pancakes."

God miraculously moved in our lives many times during our stay in Milwaukee—car problems, tire problems, financial problems, spiritual problems—God showed us time and again He would take care of us. One time when Bill planned to drive me to northern Wisconsin to counsel at a youth camp, our car had a major problem and the mechanics couldn't find the trouble. The night before we were to leave, Bill saw the entire carburetor mechanism laid out before him in a dream, with the faulty part clearly exposed. He was able to fix it the next morning and the car got me safely to camp.

When Bill came back the next week to take me home, he had a flat tire. He changed it, but we had to make the long trip relying on a badly-worn spare tire. And God. The bald tire worked just fine until we pulled safely into our own drive in Milwaukee, where it deflated with a "Hssssssss."

Financially, we were living close to the edge. Apartment rental in the big city was extremely high, and Bill's salary was only about half what he had made at Caterpillar. We budgeted very closely, but one month we made a major goof in our checking account when paying bills. We had absolutely nothing left to buy groceries for the entire month, and stretched our creativity to use whatever food we had in the house. We exchanged pop bottle deposit money for a loaf of bread and rationed our canned goods sparingly.

By the end of the month, we were down to nothing in the house to eat, nada, zip, zero, nothing. We knelt for bedtime prayers, and then I gave Billy and Mari each a spoonful of sugar to quell their tummies and tucked them into bed, hoping the sugar would suffice until Bill's paycheck came in on the first of the month.

There was a terrible winter storm that night. The wind howled and banged the shutters, and our storm door sounded like it was going to blow off its hinges. Bill went downstairs to check it and hollered, "Dollie! Come here quick!" Someone had stuck bags of groceries between the storm door and our front door, all kinds of groceries! Canned goods, baked goods, meat, fresh fruit and veggies—a veritable feast. We woke the kids up and had another prayer meeting, this time on the living room floor, praising God for His goodness.

Our time in Milwaukee had taught us that God could be counted on to do the impossible, and we blithely accepted our new financial arrangements with the RHMA as "faith missionaries." Boldly, we stepped into God's training school of faith, and continued to marvel as He provided for our daily needs in Appalachia.

With the money we had received from the sale of our furniture in Illinois, we bought a 15-year-old range and refrigerator at an auction house down in Wysock. After a lot of Ajax, elbow grease, and cold water, they looked pretty good. I figured anything would be better than the wood cook stove! The auctioneer sent us to a wholesale furniture warehouse in Elmira, New York, to pick out what we needed in the way of beds and living room furniture, then sent his son up to buy them for us on his wholesale account. We picked out the cheapest living room set they had, but when it was delivered, we discovered that Mr. Chaffee had bought us the highest priced set and only charged us for the cheap one.

That was just the beginning of God showing us all he ways He would stretch our meager funds.

Our new church had been without a pastor for a long while, but it still owed a former pastor a considerable amount of back wages. At first it was unable, or unwilling, to help us financially. But the people gave generously of their garden produce, canned goods, and meat. We often said we lived from hand to mouth—from God's hand to our mouths!

Just a week or so after we moved in, I was visiting a farm down on the Susquehanna River, helping decorate for an upcoming bridal shower. Relatives of the groom, the couple hosting the shower had stopped coming to church during the problems with the previous pastor, so we used the occasion for friendship evangelism. Before we left that afternoon, the couple agreed to return to church, and Esther even promised to teach the beginner's Sunday School class.

As we were leaving their house, Esther said, "Oh, by the way. Do you need any meat?" She handed me a big box full of ground beef and T-bone steaks! Wow! We couldn't afford T-bone steaks even when we could afford 'em! She also gave me two very nice winter suits that her son had outgrown, which fit Billy perfectly.

Two weeks into our mission adventure, we drove to Troy, New York, and spent most of our last cash on building materials for Bill's new office and $9 to have Puny's prayer letter printed. En route home, a state trooper stopped us and plied us with a barrage of questions. He asked where we lived, when we had moved there, when we were getting our vehicle and drivers' licenses, etc. He warned us we had less than two weeks left under Pennsylvania law to get new registrations.

We quickly learned that our new state had a tax-happy legislature, meaning not only did we have to pay for vehicle and drivers' licenses, we also had to get the car inspected for a fee, plus a physical exam for each of us, yet another fee. The days sped by, and still no money had arrived to get Puny legalized.

I wrote about our money woes to Mom, complaining:

> *Here it is Aug. 4, and still no check from the mission, which means there's no money there for us this month. Which also means we spent our last $5 on hamburger and bread this morning and will have to live on that until the Lord sends something our way. It's not quite as bad as it sounds, because we have the garden stuff and the things in the freezer, which we don't want to use until winter. One*

*family keeps us in potatoes and another supplies our milk.
We skim the cream off the top, shake it in a jar, and make
our own butter.*

*It's just a little unsettling to know there's no money in the
till and no definite payday to look forward to. On top of
everything else, Schmidt's cancelled our car insurance as
of yesterday, and we still haven't found an agent out here
… more expense! We both have to have a physical (and
there's some question about whether Bill's heart condition
and blood pressure will pass it) before we can get a driver's
license. Haven't got our license plates yet. We ordered them
a long time ago, but everything came back the other day—
they wanted more verification of when we bought the car.
If we bought it within a certain time before moving here,
they can make us pay 5% sales tax. Ken Buch (a fellow
missionary) had to sell his new Chevy station wagon when
he moved here from Indiana because he couldn't pay the
$250 sales tax Pennsylvania demanded.*

Like George Mueller, a great hero of the faith we admired, we
determined that we would tell no one of our financial problems and
simply trust God to provide through His people. (Obviously, I didn't
consider complaining to Mom as breaking that rule! But because
she was our greatest prayer warrior, I often shared our problems and
victories with her in my letters.) Our congregation was still deeply
in debt for expenses they had incurred under a previous pastor, and
were unable to help with the heavy gas expenses of driving long
distances daily over those mountain roads, but I'm sure they could
figure out that it financially strapped our budget.

Another one of the families who returned to the church shortly
after we called on them learned that Bill liked to build things. Dick
invited Bill up to his farm to help build a hay wagon. Bill and Billy
spent many hours working on the hay wagon, discipling Dick and

Mildred at the same time. One Sunday night, in the midst of our money woes, they invited us to "stop by the house" for a minute. Dick handed Bill $70 in cold, hard cash! Bill urged him to give it through the church, but Dick told us it was back tithes from when he wasn't going to church, and he had already told the deacons what he planned to do.

In God's gracious timing, the $70 paid for our immediate needs—the physicals, car insurance, vehicle inspection, and final utility bills we'd just received from Illinois. Now, if our mission check would come, we might have enough to get the car licensed, which, in those days, was $12.51—a huge sum when our monthly pledged support was merely $15!

Thankful for the way God had provided the night before, we eagerly approached the mailbox on Monday morning, fully anticipating the familiar envelope from the RHMA. There was one lone envelope in the box, a card from one of Bill's former co-workers. His Sunday School class had taken a love offering for us to use wherever we needed it. Enclosed was a check for $12.51, which "just happened" to be the exact amount for Puny's license, on the last day before our deadline for a license expired! Coincidence? We often said, "Coincidence is when God chooses to remain anonymous." But in this case, God wasn't anonymous—He was working through a Sunday School class!

In my next letter to Mom, I shared how God had miraculously provided for us, telling her all about how we were able to pay for our insurance and licenses. I began the letter with:

> *Shared our troubles with you last week, now I'll share our praise! Received our mission check this morning, for $70! The church gave us a $31 love offering, we got a $7 insurance refund, the dollar you sent so I could buy pineapple for Mari's pineapple bars, and another dollar from a young girl at Alta Gardens—there's a lot to praise God for! That will completely pay for the car insurance, get*

*the kids' school things, get our drivers' licenses, and buy the
pineapple! It seems when we really get in need, God lets us
stay that way for a few days to test our faith, then supplies
abundantly. It's like you said, "Praise and pray and peg
away!"*

We weren't always good students in the Training School of Faith
and often failed the test. My pregnancy and accompanying medical
bills often strained our checkbook and our faith. And my belly! Even
though the severe nausea caused me to lose weight, my figure was
being rearranged, and nothing in my wardrobe would cover that
fact. As the baby within me grew, I yearned for some nice, loose-
fitting maternity clothes.

One day, Mary Wilcox, my pregnant friend, and I drooled
over the maternity section of the Sears catalog, knowing full well
neither of us could afford to buy any new clothes. I was especially
drawn to a gorgeous blue corduroy maternity suit, one that would
cover my tummy and surround me with warmth during the coming
winter. Of course, it was out of the question, but I admit to a little
coveting.

As the problem literally grew bigger and bigger, I did something
we had promised ourselves we would never do. Our monthly mission
check was a whopping $12, not nearly enough to buy groceries and
pay the utilities, much less buy maternity clothes. So I ordered a
couple of cheap maternity dresses from the Spiegel catalog and
charged them.

That very weekend, fellow missionaries from southern
Pennsylvania came to visit and brought two boxes of slightly used
maternity clothes. I immediately wrote to cancel the order from
Spiegel's. The same day, the mailman deposited a package from Sears
at our mailbox, a package that contained the lovely blue suit I had
so admired in the catalog just a day or so earlier. What's that old
saying? "Before they call, I will answer!" I was convinced my mom

had ordered it for me, because whoever sent it had to be on God's wavelength to get exactly what I wanted.

My sister also sent me an attractive maternity outfit, and one of the church ladies bought me a lovely red jumper. Before long I had such an extensive wardrobe, I was able to share some of it with Mary. We were the best-dressed pregnant women in the neighborhood!

God even took care of my food cravings. For a long time, I had craved noodles Romanoff, but the local store didn't carry prepared foods like that. The next time we had to go to the city for a doctor appointment, I thought we'd stop at a supermarket and buy my box of noodles. Only problem was, when we were in the city, we didn't have any money. Or thought we didn't.

While searching in my purse for something else, I discovered $3 I didn't know was in there. It seems Bill had given it to me the week before to buy stuff for the church's annual harvest supper, but the local grocer gave us everything we needed, and I hadn't had to spend it. It had been so long since I'd had money in my billfold, I promptly forgot about it. What joy! Now I had enough to stop at the supermarket and pick up my box of noodles.

First, however, we went to the clinic for my prenatal checkup, and Dr. Corner gave me a prescription he said I needed right away. Precisely $3 worth of prescription, to be exact. I nearly cried ... there went my noodles Romanoff.

But the story didn't end there. When we went to pick up our kids at the Burlingames' on our way home, Mildred said, "Just a minute—I fixed a little casserole for your supper. Ain't much, just some noodles."

She didn't know it, but she sure beat Betty Crocker when it came to fixing noodles Romanoff! Hers weren't from a box, but the real old-fashioned homemade kind. We were once again reminded of Psalm 37:4: *"He shall give thee the desires of thine heart...."* Even noodles Romanoff, Lord??

Maternity dresses and noodles were one thing, but could we trust God for the enormous doctor and hospital bills we knew were headed our way with the birth of a baby? Sometimes it's easy to trust God for the small things, but somehow we think the big-ticket items are too much for Him to handle. Our income from all sources usually averaged less than $100 per month, much less than what we had earned in a week at our corporate jobs, which didn't leave much for big medical bills.

The local doctor, worried by my continuing sickness and weight loss, sent me to the Guthrie Clinic in Sayre for a thorough physical exam. Much like a smaller version of the Mayo Clinic, they put me through the most complete physical I'd ever had. I went from doctor to doctor, from test to test. The final verdict was that I was indeed 11 weeks pregnant, complicated by a badly misplaced uterus. They attempted to work it into the right position but said it would probably slip right out again anyway. They gave me the "good news" that it would cause a lot of pain and discomfort, but nothing serious.

They confirmed my local doctor's theory that the broken blood vessels in my eyes were caused by the terrible wrenching and heaving, and gave me three kinds of nausea pills. They warned me to take the medicine faithfully and to eat properly, to keep from having another marathon ordeal of nausea. Easy for them to say ... they could afford medicine and healthy food.

They also said I'd have to make frequent trips to the clinic as they "needed to keep a close watch on me." The dollar signs began to float before my eyes. How could we possibly afford all this health care?

As I passed from examining room to examining room, accompanied by all my paperwork, I noticed all the papers were flagged, "Clergy dependent." I thought that probably meant they gave some sort of discount to clergy, maybe 10 percent or something. That would help, but it would surely leave us a heap yet to pay. Then I noticed one paper marked "Insurance only."

I got up enough courage to ask the obstetrician what that meant, and he said, "If you have insurance they'll collect what they're entitled to from the insurance company. But we don't charge anything for clergy dependents. So if you don't have insurance, your baby is on us!"

What a mighty God we serve! Month after month, Satan threw discouragements and unexpected bills at us, and month after month, God miraculously supplied. Sometimes God provided through our regular supporters, but often our finances and other answers to prayer came from surprising sources. A township gravel truck sped by Puny one day on a mountain road, shattering the windshield. The county insurance refused to pay the $85.26 to get the windshield repaired, saying, "It was a normal hazard of driving." While we tried to scrape together enough to fix it, we drove around with a broken windshield. Considering it was early December and the snow was blowing in, it didn't make for a very comfortable ride in the mountains.

Our own insurance agent had earlier told us Puny wasn't covered for glass breakage and that the county should be liable. One day Bill was in the agent's office about another matter and mentioned the broken windshield again. "Oh, that reminds me," the agent said, reaching into his desk. "I checked your policy and you are covered. Here, fill in this report, and we'll get a check right off to you."

Puny got a new windshield, all the kids we continually picked up for Sunday School and Bible classes got a much warmer ride, and we got another lesson in God's Training School of Faith.

Wit-n-Wisdom: God is good all the time. He'll put food in your kitchen when you don't have a dime!

Chapter 6

Peggin' Away!

For though I be free from all men, yet have I made myself servant
unto all, that I might gain the more. I Corinthians 9:19

We soon learned that serving as a country pastor would involve much more than simply preaching on Sunday morning. The moment we drove up to our new church, we were confronted with many things that needed to be repaired—rotted steps, dirty pews, grimy windows. And, of course, the disaster of a parsonage that was to become our home. Nothing that couldn't be fixed with a little water, paint, and elbow grease, we figured, and pitched in to get both places clean and shining again.

While scrubbing months' worth of mud and barn droppings off the church floor, we discovered a strange phenomenon: the floor had a definite slope from back to front. Anything that accidentally got dropped quickly rolled to the altar area. Scrub water also puddled there, following the pull of gravity that makes water run downhill. We wondered if a crack in the foundation or a long-ago earthquake had slipped the church off its foundation, and asked our unconventional deacon, Stub, about it.

"Shucks, no, that floor was done thataway on purpose," he told us. "We figured if the church ever quit being a church, at least they couldn't sell it for a dance hall or a skatin' rink."

47

We enlisted the help of the Ladies' missionary group to help clean the church, and I was assigned to do the basement room. What a mess! Cobwebs dangled dramatically from every ceiling joist and decorated every murky corner. The cellar hadn't been touched in over eight years. I was tempted to invite the high school biology class over to collect all the bugs and spiders as a project. I found stacks of insulation board, which they'd had for eight years, planning "someday" to insulate the vestibule. Bill found window screens in the attic and proceeded to hang them at the windows, to be met with a chorus of "Why bother? Might as well wait 'til next year, now!" Obviously, the philosophy of Endless Mountain folk was: "Never do today what can wait for tomorrow."

Before we had the church and parsonage shipshape, people began calling on us for all sorts of help. "Would I mind watching their young'uns for an hour or so?" "Could the pastor take the wife and kids down to Towanda for a doctor's appointment?" Requests like that kept our phone ringing off its proverbial hook.

It also was wood bee time, and the parson was expected to help all the members get their wood supply in. In his spare time, he could get his own wood. The country mentality seemed to be that because the parson didn't have a "real job," he had nothing to do all week and was therefore at their beck and call. How hard was it to get up and preach for a half hour on Sunday morning, a short message Sunday night, and lead a prayer meetin' on Wednesday night? As they saw it, the new inhabitants in the parsonage on the hill had nothing but time on their hands and should be available to the church members in exchange for the privilege of living in that lovely house.

A few of them actually voiced these sentiments on occasion. The newness of our position perhaps made us impervious to such remarks, and we accepted our job as errand boys and general flunkies with glee. We wanted to be like those suffering saints in Hebrews 10, who "took joyfully the spoiling of their goods, knowing they had in heaven a better and enduring substance."

Bill figured it was a good way to get to know our people, see the beautiful countryside, and show by example God's mercy and compassion. His spouse, on the other hand, sometimes related more to the admonishment in Hebrews 10:36, "You have need of patience that, after you have done the will of God, you might receive the promise."

Many a night I put the kids in bed, then sat up for hours waiting for Bill to come driving home from sitting with a sick person, helping deliver a calf, counseling parents about their wayward teens, or meeting with the deacons about church business. Most of the men were dairy farmers who didn't get in from the barns until late evening, which meant most of Bill's house calls couldn't begin until after 8 p.m. Considering that our "parish" encircled many, many miles of mountain hamlets with our congregation scattered across all those miles, it was no wonder that Bill often didn't get home until after midnight on most nights.

I often expressed my worries in letters to Mom that I wrote while waiting for Bill to get home, sometimes voicing my fears that he'd gone off a cliff or into a ditch on the slippery roads, especially when the clock ticked closer and closer to midnight. Early in December, I wrote:

> *Sure hope we are able to come home for Christmas so Bill can rest up. He's just going round the clock, and it's beginning to show on him. The poor guy is always out splitting wood or something, and hasn't got a decent night's sleep in weeks. Right now he's over at Wilcoxes' trying to get some wood in the snow (and it's pitch dark besides). We used our very last log this afternoon.*
>
> *He's also helping George track down a lost cow. She was due to freshen today, and they're afraid she's hiding her calf out in the woods. As dark and slippery as it is, they're going to be looking a long time. When he gets done there, he has to drive Lee over to Columbia Crossroads to tow home*

their car that broke down. I'm also out of medicine again, but don't know when there'll be time to go up after it. It's 7 o'clock now, and we haven't had supper yet.

Bill does an awful lot for these folks, but I think they appreciate it. I was thrilled Sunday night when Lee got up and thanked the Lord for "a pastor who loved his people so much he'd stand out in a driving rain storm helping them buy a car."

Be back in a minute ... smells like my potatoes just burned up! Sure wish Bill and Billy would get home ... I'm getting hungry! Bill just called from Wilcoxes' to tell me how to operate the dampers to keep the fire going. They still haven't found the heifer or the calf, so they're going back out again. She's worth about $350, so naturally they're pretty anxious to find her. They're afraid she slipped on the ice and broke a leg or something, which would really be rough. It's too late, too, to get my medicine. Hope I get through the night without the nausea getting started again.

Meanwhile, it's freezing in here. I'm not much of a fire builder, especially with nothing but green wood. Incidentally, if you sent that blue maternity dress, thanks a lot. But if you did, you shouldn't have, because you can't afford it any more than we can! We love you!

* * *

Just a few days later, I wrote home again, still complaining about the bad roads and our busy schedule.

Dear Mom — Guess there's time for a few lines while Bill is getting ready to go. It's a nasty night here, snow, sleet, wind, and rain, and I'd like nothing better than to curl up by the stove and relax. But some folks wanted to talk to us tonight, so off we go. And here's Bill—if we get home early enough, I'll try to finish this.

Later. Well, it's not early, but maybe I can write while the kids get their baths. Went to the family with all the boys, then to visit the Cranes, and here it is nearly 10 o'clock. Another evening of ministry, and none of my housework even started. Spent the morning at Teacher's Training with CEF in Athens, then took my Smithfield kids to my Milan club this afternoon for a special missionary speaker from Ireland. The county director brought her Athens club down, too, so we really had a houseful of kids. Miss Daugherty, the missionary, will be speaking at our church tomorrow night, and our young people are in charge of the meeting. Had 32 teens out last week, so are expecting a good crowd tomorrow night.

Been raining steady for several hours. When it freezes tonight, things are really going to be treacherous. Have to take Levia over to Troy in the morning to get a loan for a car, so I'm hoping the roads aren't too bad. Their car broke down last week, so Bill has been playing chauffeur—also to the Nelsons, whose car went kaput. Bill's taken Mr. Nelson back and forth to work and to get his car, and driven Lee home from work a couple of times, plus doing all their other driving.

He took Lee grocery shopping the other day, and Lee put a small sack in the backseat for us. Turned out to be 5 pounds of sugar, the one thing we'd forgotten to get earlier. When Bill asked Lee how he knew we needed sugar, Lee answered, "The Lord told me to get you some sugar." Call it coincidence, or what you will, but it happens too many times to be chance.

Did I tell you Bonnie Nelson came forward Sunday? Also Diane, our wild and wooly one! Soon as we got home from church, Mabel Wilcox called to relate a strange incident. On her way home, she noticed an attractive young woman walking along the dirt road, all dressed up. When she offered her a ride, the woman replied, "No thanks, I'm waiting for Rev. Farley." We figured it must have been someone who knew Bill took the Nelson kids home that way, but this particular Sunday they rode home with George and Mary. To satisfy our curiosity, we drove over to Nelsons and learned she's Mrs. Nelson's divorced sister who came to live with them. She walked all the way into E. Smithfield to church, but was real anxious to meet us and hoped we'd come along the road. She was saved years ago, but just came back to the Lord recently. That night she came to our church with us and gave a wonderful testimony of how the Lord delivered her from cigarettes just three weeks ago. She just bubbles over, and is really happy to have found a Bible-preaching church. She's also a good influence on Mrs. Nelson (a good Christian who doesn't come to church and has a very rough life).

Bill got to talk to Mr. Nelson quite a bit while driving him back and forth to work. He was saved in 1934 but has really been on the skids with liquor. They've been on relief for years, and he just recently got a good job at Ingersoll-Rand and is trying to stay sober. Then his car broke down, and he was worried sick he'd lose his new job. He has such a poor work record, he was afraid they'd think he was drinking again. God is really working in that family, and we expect to see them all at church regularly from now on.

Better quit yakking and get my bath while the bathroom is warm for a change. After we take Levia to Troy, we promised to drive her and Mildred up to Elmira to the day-old bakery sales.

P.S. Mari was in her glory this week. Someone gave us a box of groceries, including a jar of homemade strawberry jam, "just like Granma makes!" Needless to say, it didn't last long!

* * *

Puny explained our hectic schedule in his November prayer letter, "Saga of the Missionary Lark, Part 6" —

These people must think I'm a truck, instead of a compact little Lark! Someone anonymously sent Mr. Farley one hundred dollars for a chain saw, and he's been working it and me to death ever since. Every few days he loads me up with oilcan, chain saw, gas can and tool kit, then off we go where fools fear to tread. Actually, if you think the roads here are bad, you should be along when he turns me off the roads and heads over snow and ice into the woods, to parts unknown. After he and the chain saw have had a good work out, he loads me up from stem to stern with piles of wood. Then, if we're lucky enough to get out of the woods and back to the road, we head for home.

But still no rest for the weary. Mrs. Farley is usually standing impatiently at the door, coat and boots in hand, waiting for her turn at me. She loads me up with easel, flannel board, and who-knows-what, along with a pile of kids, and off we go to one of her Bible clubs.

When we get home from there, I get to rest a few minutes while they gulp down some supper, then off we go again. On youth nights, I spend about an hour and a half picking up teenagers and an equal time taking 'em back home. On other nights, I usually just take Mr. Farley calling, no small feat in this ice and snow.

Once in awhile, there's real excitement—like when the phone rings and the Farleys come running wildly out, and we're off to a fire. Once, it was to the Wilcoxes where they had a bad chimney fire; another time to the Burlingames where Richard was burned quite badly in a gasoline fire.

I'm not really complaining, though, 'cause this winter driving really gets interesting sometimes. Like when I got gas line freeze-up and had to be towed for miles by a Jeep. Come to think of it, that was just a little humiliating! Then there was the time I had a load of giggling girls, met another vehicle in a very strategic spot and had to back all the way down a winding, icy, mountain road without backup lights. You should have heard the squeals!!

Or the other night when me and two buddies took 29 young people all the way down to Franklindale to hear the new RHMA evangelists ... that was some night! The kids were loaded in us like sardines; I got nervous and slipped on the ice, fishtailing twice; then we couldn't find a gas station open, and I had to come all the way back on an empty tank. Oh well, it's all in a day's work.

* * *

Wit-n-Wisdom: If you want to be great in God's Kingdom, you've got to be the servant of all.

CHAPTER 7

Past Glory and Future Work

Go ye into all the world and preach the Gospel to every creature. Mark 16:15

One day late in August, a young man came to visit, bringing his mother and his fiancé. He told us he had grown up in Riggs, along with eight brothers and sisters, and was now a student at Columbia Bible College, under appointment to Malaysia with Overseas Mission Fellowship, formerly the China Inland Mission. Wow! A missionary from our tiny country church?

"My dad was a baker here in Riggs and was saved at this church. Many years ago he felt God calling him to missions, so he packed up all nine of us kids and headed for Bolivia, where we've been ever since, working among the Trinitario Indians," John said.

During our conversation with John, we learned that all nine of the Snyder children were currently serving as missionaries or in training. His older brother Joe was a missionary with the Trinitario Indians and was back in the States to attend the New Tribes Mission Bible School in Wisconsin before returning to Bolivia. John asked if Joe could have a service at our church and report to the congregation. Jumping at the opportunity to re-introduce our people to missions, we quickly booked him for the following week and immediately began to get notices in all the papers and area radio stations.

Sunday night, the churchyard was full, and the road was jammed with cars parked on both sides for blocks. We brought in every chair on the premises and still had standing room only, with people in the vestibule and standing outside looking in the windows. The Snyder family were local celebrities, and our evening's speaker had been speaking daily on WPEL for a couple of weeks. Horace Snyder, father of the family, and several brothers and sisters came to the service as well. It seemed everybody in the region was there to welcome the Snyders back home.

After Joe shared his message, he remarked, "Just think, because this little country church was faithful in proclaiming the Gospel, over 500 Trinitario Indians in Bolivia now know Christ as their Savior!" I looked over at Bill and could almost see him mentally flipping through the Bible School enrollment, wondering which of these children would be missionaries in a few years.

Apparently, our church had not always been a discouraged, tiny congregation on the verge of closing its doors. What had happened to bring them down so far they needed a missionary pastor themselves? We determined to find the answer to that perplexing question and discovered there were dozens of folks from Riggs in full-time Christian work. In addition to the Snyder family, there were several pastors and pastors' wives, fifteen or so missionaries, several Bible college teachers, and a couple of radio ministers. We had a brainstorming session with our folks, asking them to remember as many workers as they could who had once been a part of our church. They came up with a staggering list of 40-some people who were now out in the far-flung fields of the world. I think the number even surprised them!

While we couldn't pinpoint a specific time the ministry had begun to go downhill, a pattern of neglect emerged. In one of the country's financial crises, the dairy economy also crashed, and people quit giving to the church. With the budget going south, the first thing to be dropped was missionary support.

It became a vicious cycle—the less they sent to missions, the further the total income dropped, until finally it reached the stage when we came on the scene, where they didn't have enough income to pay the utility bills, buy supplies, or pay a pastor, and were about to close the church doors.

In his straightforward manner, Bill addressed the problem head on. With full assurance that we were absolutely in the place God wanted us, he preached the Word and trusted the Lord to bear fruit. Our agreement with the church was that we were there on a six-month trial, and if they didn't like us, they could vote us out after the trial period. Occasionally, Stub would caution Bill, "Better not preach too strong, or we'll vote you out!" He always had a smile on his face when he said things like that, and we didn't take it too seriously.

One of the ladies said that if the former pastor had preached the sermons Bill was preaching, the folks would have walked out on him. "Yet the stronger you preach, the better they treat you," she added. Actually, I didn't think he was preaching strong at all, just hammering away at their need to get out and witness and win others, and to support missions.

It began to bear fruit, and one of our greatest thrills was when one dear lady raised her hand for prayer that she might be a soul winner. A wonderful, mild lady, she was rather quiet and shy, letting her boisterous husband do all the talking. She further surprised us when she asked Bill to baptize her. She had been baptized as a young child, and in the past had never seen the need for believer's baptism.

Small steps of spiritual growth among our folks continued to encourage us. At a Wednesday night service, one of the ladies suggested that some of the folk go to call on her neighbor who had cancer, then promptly offered to go with me the next day. Some of the deacons began going on calls with Bill, and of course, church attendance began to grow.

Bill saw the need to establish a church budget and challenged the people to give the first 10 percent of all church offerings to missions. Instead of asking them for a set salary, he suggested that the pastor be given a percentage of what was left after the mission 10 percent. They quickly saw the wisdom in that idea, as it meant they wouldn't have to struggle to meet a set salary, remembering the huge amount they still owed the former pastor. Because we had our missionary supporters back in Illinois, we weren't dependent on the church for our income, and this arrangement freed them from financial worries.

It didn't do much for our personal finances, however. At times when we had to be gone from the field, we paid our own pulpit supply. I remember several times when Bill was ill and I had to call in a replacement speaker. The set fee back then was $15 per service, so I wrote the speaker's check from our personal checkbook, trying hard to smile when the treasurer gave me our week's salary .... $2.50!

At our first quarterly business meeting the clerk reported that attendance averaged 33 in morning service for the three months we had been there. A youth group was started, averaging more than 25 every Friday night. The first VBS they had tried in several years enrolled over 70 kids, and two Good News Clubs were begun in East Smithfield and Milan. Not great statistics relative to large city churches, but big strides forward in a small mountain community like Riggs.

Were these people any less deserving of the Gospel than their city counterparts? Did God love them less because they lived miles from a large city church?

No, no, a thousand times no! The more we worked with our mountain folk, the more our burden for rural America grew. We knew there were thousands of such places across the United States, remote areas that would never hear the Gospel unless someone went off the beaten path and took it to them. We determined more than ever to throw our hearts and lives into this ministry.

Even though we were small in number, we would give it 100%. Our Christmas programs, youth meetings and activities, Kid's Clubs—everything we did—received the best we had within us. As we cleaned and polished the church, put fresh flowers on the altar every week, washed the windows till they sparkled, and "preached our hearts out," we did it all for the glory of God.

Attendance continued to climb, new people joined the church, and numbers accepted Jesus and decided to follow Him. Things were looking up at Grace Baptist Church in Riggs, PA.

And Satan took notice.

Wit-n-Wisdom: The best remedy for a sick church is to put it on a missionary diet.

CHAPTER 8

Home for Christmas

*Fear not, for, behold, I bring you good tidings of great
joy, which shall be to all people... Luke 2:10*

Winter hit with a vengeance in the Endless Mountains. The vista from our mountaintop was awe-inspiring, the view that Christmas cards are made of. A Christmas addict all my life, I could hardly wait for the season, dreaming of all those holiday scenes depicted on the cards—glowing fireplace bedecked with greens and holly, hung with stockings, in a delightfully clean room. Ah, yes, the parsonage would glow with the season this year!

Once again my reality check bounced. I've yet to see a Christmas card scene that depicts the reality of living with a wood stove. A worn-out housewife in a worn-out robe trudging outside every hour on the hour to lug in an armful of fuel for the log-hungry monster. Or that same housewife continually sweeping up tons of bark, wood chips, and ashes that somehow manage to sprawl across the hearth. Or that same housewife, dust rag in hand, forever chasing the dust and soot that filter out of nowhere to land on every knick-knack and Christmas ornament in the place.

My Christmas dreaming turned into a nightmare of furniture covered with dust, floors covered with wood chips, robes covered with black soot. The dust and soot got so bad I had to urge the kids, "Hurry up and eat your soup while it's still clean." Even my new Christmas slippers had soot-covered toes where I used them to try to kick in the logs that were invariably too big for the opening in the stove.

My worst nightmare, however, was seeing my young husband aging before my eyes, getting physically exhausted from all the wood chopping and gathering chores. The doctor's early warning so many years earlier haunted me. Was he doing too much? Would his heart really give out? Falling into bed after midnight every night, I'd lie there listening to Bill's heart pounding, sometimes so hard it literally shook the bed. His blood pressure generally hovered around 200, a fact that scared me. I tried to help with the wood chores as often as I could, but my advancing pregnancy put a stop to that.

All the romantic scenarios showed Christmas pictures of cozy farmhouses, windows ablaze with light, snow on the roof and surrounding landscape shrubs. I often wondered how the words "cozy" and "farmhouse" ever got linked together. I could think of a lot of four-letter words to describe our farmhouse parsonage, but "cozy" certainly wasn't one of them. The wind howled through the cracks around the windows and doors, bringing with it icy slivers of snow. Whatever heat we managed to generate in the wood stove wafted its way breezily out through those same cracks. Billy's bed was often covered with snow that blew in. Finally it got so bad, we closed off his room and made him a bed on the living room couch.

Like the peasants during the Dark Ages before central heating, we kept warm by the crude methods primitive man used: gathering round a fire and wrapping ourselves in heavy cloaks.

We also had our own version of the Victorian Yule log. As the fire died to romantic embers and the quilt no longer warmed us, I often turned to Bill and murmured, "Yule have to go get another log for the fire!"

As a country-girl wannabe, I had always filled my home with the nostalgia-inducing scents of what I imagined a country Christmas to be … the spicy aroma of wassail, cinnamon, fresh-baked cookies, turkey baking, fresh pine and holly berries, chestnuts roasting over an open fire. I bought every scent-producing candle, cleaner, or potpourri I could find to send those artificial fragrances wafting through my house at Christmastime.

Our first Christmas in the farmlands of northern Pennsylvania burst that scented bubble in a hurry. The ever-present smell of wood smoke, and damp leaves that we constantly tracked in while getting the wood, permeated the air, blotting out any delightful candle scents I managed to produce. And who could forget the stench of the outhouses and chicken coops everywhere we went to call? Morning barn chores before church left an essence that lingered on the farmers' clothes; the barn droppings that clung to their shoes carried their own malodorous message.

When I wrinkled up my nose at the smells, Bill reminded me of the first Christmas. "What do you suppose it was like for Joseph and Mary in the stable?"

In his best poetic style, Bill preached to me. "Think about it. What were the real scents of Christmas? I'm quite sure the newborn Savior wasn't greeted with the enticing aura of wassail, pine boughs, and apple pie. His tiny nose was doubtless assaulted by the fetid stench of manure, animal bodies, and musty manger straw. Months later, when the Wise Men made their appearance, they brought frankincense and myrrh to sweeten His way, but even these were symbols of burial." Bill paused just long enough to make sure my eyes hadn't glazed over, then continued, "Like the Wise Men, we can sweeten the way of the Christ child. Rev. 5:8 says our prayers are presented to Him in 'golden vials full of odors.'"

Never one to pass up an opportunity for an object lesson, my preacher husband challenged me, "Instead of complaining about the smells, we need to pray that our lives will be a sacrifice of a 'sweet-smelling savor' to Christ."

One major sacrifice I was not quite ready to make was spending Christmas away from home. Like other "displaced persons," most missionaries live hundreds, if not thousands, of miles away from family and seldom get to go home for the holidays. Both Bill and I had close-knit, loving families, and every year we knocked ourselves out to take in all the celebrations and traditions of both families.

Now, six months into our first mission field, we faced the prospect of missing all those traditional family gatherings for the first time. Instead, we would be celebrating in an unfamiliar environment amidst cultural customs that were strange to us, not with relatives and close friends, but probably at home alone with our two kids. Homesickness surrounded us with a vengeance, and we yearned for a familiar face, a familiar hearth, and a familiar hug.

We were scheduled to go back to our annual mission conference in April and tried to console ourselves that it would only be a few more months before we would see the folks at home. Then my obstetrician, Dr. Corner, dashed those hopes. "There's no way you're going to be able to travel that close to your delivery date," he warned. "If you want to travel, you'd better get it done now."

Maybe we should go home for Christmas? The possibility was enticing, but not probable. Money was scarcer than hen's teeth, and so much holiday activity had been planned at the church we would be too busy to leave for a week or so.

As Christmas drew nearer, however, it began to look like we might get to make the trip. We had the church Christmas program, caroling at the Senior Citizens' Center, our young people's party, and the kids' school program all planned early so we could take a few days off.

But money was still a major problem. There were only a few days left until departure time, and we had no idea how we would finance the trip. Our monthly support check from the mission board was overdue, and we hoped it was because of the poor mail delivery system. It was unthinkable that our faithful supporters had overlooked their pledges at Christmas! We pinned all our hopes on our mission check getting to us in time. We prayed fervently that the mailman could make it over the snowbound roads.

With great eagerness, we plowed through the snowdrifts to the mailbox every morning, hounding the mailman. But day after day passed with no mission check. Still praying for a miracle, we went ahead and packed for the trip.

In anticipation of leaving on Sunday after the morning service, we hosted the young people's Christmas party on Friday night. A telephone call Saturday shredded any hope for our trip. "Barbie didn't come home from your party last night," the caller said. "Do you know where she is?"

We spent a frantic day trying to find her, chasing down every rumor as to her possible whereabouts. In desperation, we called the police, who finally traced her to a jail down in West Virginia. Fifteen-year-old Barbie had met a fellow somewhere after our party, ran away with him, and was picked up 800 miles away for vagrancy.

Her parents were unable to drive down to get her, and she refused to come home without her boyfriend. We ran up a frightful phone bill trying to persuade her to come home, but with no luck. It looked like the only solution was for us to make the trip ourselves, using what little cash we had for the gas. Our long-prayed-for vacation in Illinois was definitely out of the question now.

We made one last desperate phone call to the West Virginia jail, offering to wire the money for the boy's bus ticket if they would promise to come home. When the wayward couple finally agreed to this, we took every cent we had to the telegraph office for the tickets.

Our Sunday departure day came and went, but we hung onto one last shred of hope. Just possibly if we waited for the mailman Monday morning, there was still one more chance for God to answer our prayers to go home for Christmas, one more chance for that mission check to come. We just about ambushed the mailman Monday morning. Sure enough, there was the familiar envelope from the mission office.

Our excitement crashed to the ground as we opened the long-awaited envelope. $5! Hardly enough to finance a trip from Pennsylvania to Illinois. Apparently our supporters had forgotten us.

Still not willing to accept defeat, I asked hopefully, "Maybe there's something else in the mail?"

Bill's glum expression matched my own as he shook his head and held up a handful of mail. "No, nothing but these Christmas cards."

Overwhelmed by disappointment, I burst into tears while Bill began to open the cards. Suddenly, it began to "rain money." Dollar bills and checks fell out of every card we opened. $1, $5, $10! The Christmas cards yielded nearly $200, more money than we had seen in a long, long time. Once again, God had heard the cry of our heart, understood our yearning, and proved His faithfulness.

Wit-n-Wisdom: In your worst of times, remember God's message of Christmas—help is on the way!

CHAPTER 9

Trials and Triumphs

"Knowing this, that the trying of your faith works patience." James 1:3

Traveling between Pennsylvania and Illinois was never easy, considering the heavy traffic on Interstate 94, the huge 18-wheelers that barreled down the highway overtaking everything in their path, and the howling winds that blew constantly off the Great Lakes. We were so excited about going home for Christmas, however, the hazards of travel barely phased us. We stopped in Detroit to spend the night with Bill's aunt and uncle and were happily surprised when they took Puny to get a grease job and oil change.

That was only the beginning of gifts for our little missionary Lark. When we got to East Peoria, we found a Christmas card for Puny under the tree from one of my brothers-in-law, good for a complete tune-up. Others gave him money for gas, for a baby car seat, and for other imaginative "car" gifts.

Puny wasn't the only one who received gifts. It seems everywhere we went someone loaded us down with gifts—clothing and other presents for us and the kids plus groceries, tools, a lantern, from Alta Gardens Baptist Church; quilts and a baby shower from Chillicothe Bible Church; and numerous cash gifts from other churches. It was thrilling to see how many people were following our missionary exploits and praying for us. No wonder God was mightily blessing the work!

The trip to Illinois buoyed our spirits and encouraged us to get back on the field and tackle whatever Satan sent our way. The day after New Year's, we left Peoria during a horrendous rainstorm, which followed us all the way to Buffalo, where it turned into a frightful winter storm. The snow came down so fast, our wipers couldn't keep it off the windshield, and Bill had to drive with the window open, sticking his arm out every few seconds to manually clear the windshield.

The wind howled, buffeting Puny all over the road, threatening to tear the cartop carrier off his roof. We began to think we'd never get home, but we finally made it very late Saturday night. We were totally exhausted from the nightmarish trip, but the worst was yet to come.

As we walked into our kitchen, I let out a shriek. "Oh, no!" I cried, as I slipped on the icy floor. The water heater, which we had drained and shut off before we left, had apparently been plugged with rust, and hadn't drained completely. The plug froze and broke loose, pouring water all over the kitchen floor. Of course, with no heat in the house, the flood froze, so we had a virtual rusty ice rink in our kitchen.

After mopping and soaking up water most of the night, we tried to get a couple hours' sleep before church the next morning. More discouragement. We had a record-breaking ceremony, but not on the high side. We had a little contest going—If the attendance ever reached 70, the Sunday School superintendent would break a record over Bill's head; if it dropped to 15, Bill would break a record on the superintendent's head. That morning, a tired and frazzled preacher cracked a 78-rpm on Lee's noggin. It seems everyone else decided to take a vacation while the pastor was gone, and only four or five people bothered to come to church.

One of the few who did show up was the girl who had caused us such distress before Christmas. She brought along a lovely mixing bowl set and a card for us as a Christmas gift from her folks in appreciation of Bill's help in finding her and getting things straightened out in their family.

Perhaps from the stress of the trip or cleaning up the water, I had another severe bout of nausea and could barely function for days. Mari came down with a bad earache and swollen glands, and Bill was so sick by Tuesday he couldn't go out and hunt up more wood. Using our Christmas money, we broke down and ordered a small load of coal.

Ah, sweet warmth! Pure bliss! The coal made the house much warmer, and coal fires lasted a lot longer than the fast-burning wood. For the first time since we had moved in to the parsonage, our house actually felt hot. It was so good to go home after church to a warm house.

Our coal supply didn't last long. Bill felt well enough by the end of the week to get out into the woods to cut more fuel. He went out to see if the road was clear enough for him to get back in and load the wood he had already cut, but he realized he would need to borrow Stub's tractor with chains. First, he had to help Stub spread manure before he could use the tractor. A fierce wind was blowing, and the snow was drifting while Bill worked to keep his family warm—certainly not what the doctor had ordered.

It sleeted constantly that weekend, leaving a load of ice blanketing the already packed snow. Then we got more snow, more freezing rain, and back to snow. The roads were all but impassable, and church attendance understandably dropped. Sunday night, we drove down to the church and nobody else showed up. At 8:30 we decided to go back home. Just as we got into our car, the Wilcoxes pulled up, so we went ahead and had church. They lived the farthest away from the church and made it with no trouble, while everyone else stayed home and watched television. A few weeks like that, and we were getting downright discouraged.

In pastoral training classes, we had been warned about the "honeymoon period" when a pastor takes a new church. We hadn't counted on our honeymoon ending so abruptly, however. What once had been so delightfully charming and unique to us now became a drudge, a duty, and sometimes downright distasteful. I no longer giggled as I tried to get a tiny smelt or other strange critter past my taste buds. Instead, I gagged. Hauling wood or digging out of ditches lost the romance of living in the past; now it was a rite of survival.

Our people, likewise, suffered the pangs of a love becoming routine. Where once the crazy foibles of the city slickers in the parsonage had been a constant source of amusement, now they were fuel for gossip and complaints. Perhaps it was Bill's failing health, coupled with my unending morning sickness, added to incessant bad weather. Whatever the cause, the honeymoon was definitely over. We and our people settled into a rut of complaints, discouragement, and low attendance.

Early in January, it began raining. It rained for days, melting away most of the snow. The wet pavements and gravel roads froze solid each night, making driving especially hazardous. Driving the school bus, Stub often had to back down our road, gun the engine, and make a run for the steep hill. Sometimes he couldn't make it, and the kids had to walk, or slide, down to catch the bus at the bottom of the hill.

One evening, friends invited Bill to a meeting in Towanda, and as they tried to climb our hill, they had a flat tire. Then they got stuck in our drive, which was nearly impassable. What should have been a pleasant evening of fellowship turned into another nightmare of digging and pushing for Bill, another blow to his weakening heart. A fellow pastor gave us a set of chains for Puny, making our nightly visits a little easier, and at least we could get out our drive without getting stuck.

From the time we began our work in the mountains, the area had suffered a severe drought. When we couldn't find enough water for our first baptismal service, we joked, "Water is so scarce here, we may have to baptize our converts by dunking. We've heard some of the other Baptist have gone to sprinkling, and the Presbyterians are dry cleaning." The weeks of pouring rain didn't help the drought situation much, and even those among us who had indoor plumbing were faced with pipes and faucets that refused to deliver water from empty wells.

We began to think that our church folks, too, were "empty wells without water." The slightest provocation, be it bad weather or bad attitudes, kept them from church, and attendance, or lack thereof, kept us discouraged. Two of the families who had returned to the church and had provided some of our greatest moral support got miffed at us for some reason and stopped coming again. Bill took Rev. Longenecker's advice and kept on loving them, continuing to run errands for them, fixing their cars, and even giving one family Puny's new overload springs to use.

Rev. Longenecker's advice worked. We hadn't been home a week before the families were all smiles and helpfulness again. They came over to help with the young people's group, bringing us a big hunk of beef and some surplus cheese. We took both women to Elmira to shop the next day and gave one of them the frozen turkey that Kennedy's Market had put in our Christmas basket before we left town. She promptly invited us to come for dinner the next Sunday, where we dined on roast turkey and all the trimmings.

But other things began to wear us down. For our first weeks, we had to drive out to the Wilcox farm to do laundry. Then missionaries who were returning to the field in Africa gave us a Maytag wringer washer that someone had given them while they were on home assignment. The parsonage wasn't set up for laundry facilities, but we devised an arrangement in the bathroom where I could hook up a hose at the faucet to fill the machine. After getting the contraption all set up, I'd stand there for hours running clothes through the wringer into the bath tub, where we swished them around to rinse. Often, Mari helped by sitting on the toilet seat, handing the rinsed pieces for me to run them back through the wringer into a basket. It provided wonderful mother/daughter time, as she entertained me with her creative story telling and singing. We'd make the chore less stressful by pretending we were running a Chinese laundry during the Gold Rush or doing laundry along the Oregon Trail.

Sometimes I longed for the good old days when doing laundry simply meant picking up Bill's clean, ironed shirts at the dry cleaners or baskets of neatly folded laundry from the local Laundromat.

Now, in addition to all the work with the wringer machine, laundry also involved lugging the heavy wet clothes outside to the clothesline. I'd stoop and bend, stoop and bend, all the while dodging the hornets, wasps, and bees that buzzed around my head. Billy got stung a few times while helping me and developed a bad allergy to the stings.

On bright sunny days, I didn't mind hanging the clothes out. I loved the smell of fresh sheets and towels. But how do you get eight or ten loads of laundry dry on all those rainy or snowy days? Our living room began to look like a Chinese laundry, with clotheslines strung from corner to corner, from pillar to post. Anyone who happened by on laundry day was in grave danger of getting slapped or strangled by dangling wet underwear.

And, of course, all that laundry had to be ironed and folded. That was before Perma-press had been discovered, so I always had huge baskets of laundry waiting for the ironing board.

The week we returned from our Christmas trip, I had eleven loads of laundry piled up. By evening, my back was so bent over from working the wringer, I could barely stand up for my Teacher Training class in Sayre. "There's only one reason I'd want to be rich—so I could buy a washer and dryer!" I complained to Bill. "I can't think of anything that would make my life easier." What did women do before the advent of automatic washers and dryers?

Early on in our ministry, we realized the importance of fellowship with other pastors and sought out those in our area of similar theological persuasion. We longed for camaraderie, not conflict, and figured pastors with our own evangelical bent would be a good place to start. And how we needed fellow pastors and wives to commiserate with!

We met monthly with a group of Baptist and Bible church pastors across the northern tier of Pennsylvania and the southern tier of New York. This often meant a good deal of driving, since we were widely scattered from Corning, Elmira, and Waverly, New York, to Athens, Towanda, and Sayre, Pennsylvania.

Shortly after Christmas, we drove to Horseheads, New York, for lunch with eight other couples in the ministry. Listening to all their prayer requests and woes, it seemed like Satan was working overtime in all of our churches. Bill and I discovered our problems were minor compared with some of theirs. God used these pastoral "gripe and praise sessions" to encourage us to keep on keeping on. We weren't in this battle alone.

On my 28th birthday, the weather broke loose again with fury. Cold, icy, and rainy with a wind howling fiercely through the house. We tried in vain to get a fire going with the green wood we had left in the garage. Dick had shown Bill earlier where to get some good-burning pine roots. Suited up in parka and boots, Bill determined to go out in the storm for fuel. Against my pleas not to go, he spent the day "playing" with Stub's tractor and wagon, then loaded up a huge wagon full of wood.

His work paid off warmly. The fire burned very hot and smelled great. The combination of the pine roots and green wood together made a wonderful fire and kept us warm throughout the rest of the storm.

My birthday breakfast consisted of government surplus meat, as the larder was nearly empty again. It actually wasn't too bad, because USDA had put out a new issue without mutton, and it was much easier to get down. I eagerly anticipated my birthday supper. Mildred had invited us up to celebrate and had cornered the kids to find out all my favorite foods. The best cook in the neighborhood, Mildred outdid herself for my birthday supper, serving us a gastronomical delight.

The next afternoon, my ever-present morning sickness hit again with a vengeance. I tried to get somebody to take over my Girl Scouts for me, but no one was willing. When I got there and saw a beautiful birthday cake, ice cream, and presents, I was really glad I hadn't found a substitute. The refreshments only stayed down until I got home to barf in the bathroom, but it would have been an awful disappointment to the girls if I hadn't showed up after all their work.

Even though we weren't dairy farmers and didn't own a single cow, the Milk Inspectors ruled a big part of our time. When our people spoke of the Milk Inspectors, it was in capital letters and hushed voices. Those guys were almost as feared as Russia's KGB. Whenever someone saw an MI in the neighborhood, he'd rush in to call and warn all the nearby farmers, giving them time to clean the milkers, chase the chickens out of the milkhouse, and pitch the manure out the back door in a mad frenzy before the MI made it to their farm.

Bill was often called upon to help someone appease the MIs, doing everything from clipping cows to pitching manure. The day after we'd enjoyed such a delightful birthday supper with Dick and Mildred Burlingame, Dick asked Bill to help him put a new roof on his milk house. The MI had ordered the new roof and insisted it had to be installed pronto or Dick's farm wouldn't pass inspection.

We also were keeping busy with the official duties of ministry—despite the financial doldrums of winter. A church at Quackenbush Hill was interested in becoming part of the RHMA. Since we were closer to it than the field director, we became the go-between, driving up to answer questions, meet with church leaders, and explain mission policies.

To prepare for our annual evangelistic meetings, the church ladies spent a lot of time helping us clean the church. I didn't have enough money to buy rug shampoo that day, so the next day we drove over near Troy to our church treasurer's house to get an advance for the shampoo, came home and sprinkled Glamorene over the carpet, then returned before prayer meeting to vacuum it. In the meantime, I baked a big batch of cookies to take when we visited a new neighbor.

We also baked a surprise birthday cake for Mildred, the lady who never forgot anyone else's special days. All this during the lowest financial month we'd endured to date! Talking to our fellow missionaries, we all decided that supporters tend to forget about their commitments during the rough winter months.

Down in Oregon Hill, the Matthewsons, our field directors, were having a rough time, too. Maynard told us he had to turn down speaking engagements because they didn't have enough money for gas to get there. At a pastor's meeting the week before, our missionary from Windham Summit was really down in the dumps. He cancelled their evening services and was about to submit his resignation.

We had used our entire church check to pay the light company to keep them from turning off our electricity, leaving us not a red cent to live on. In desperation, we charged $8 worth of groceries at Kennedy's Market to get the things for Mildred's party.

Bill's heart condition had worsened to the point he couldn't lie down in the bed but had to sit up all night in order to breathe. The doctors at Mayo Clinic had warned him that was a bad sign to look out for, that it signified he was going into heart failure. He made an appointment with a heart specialist at the Guthrie Clinic in Sayre but still refused to slow down.

Despite all our worries and woes, and because so many people back home were praying for us, the Lord continued to buoy us up spiritually. Church attendance picked up sharply. Bill was doing a series of radio messages for Bible Lighthouse, which broadcast over "Light for the Valley" each morning. His broadcasts no doubt helped advertise our presence throughout the area.

The wild teenager we had held out so little hope for became the star of our quiz team and enrolled in the mission's Bible correspondence course. Another finally licked his battle with drugs and became a regular at all our meetings. The youth group itself grew from zero to more than 30 in just a few short weeks, giving us a vibrant, active bunch of teens. On the other side of the generation gap, a 73-year-old woman, who declared "I've never taught a class in my entire life," volunteered to teach the Beginners Class. Visitors appeared in our services nearly every week, and many of them liked what they saw and stayed.

When our six-month trial period was up, the congregation voted unanimously to keep us on. As in marriages, the proverbial billing and cooing had stopped, but in its place was a deep-seated love for each other, a love that would survive the onslaughts of Satan. And, as in most marriages, the "billing" went on forever! There was much work to be done, and God had no one but us ill-equipped people to do it. Together, we would get the job done.

Someone once said the Lord created the world in six days and rested on the seventh. On the eighth day, He started answering complaints. Once we were firmly ensconced as the permanent pastor, the complaints started rolling in.

Wit-n-Wisdom: If you don't like the bleatings of sheep, you shouldn't be a shepherd.

Bill and Dollie

Billy and Mari

Johnny, Jeff, and Margie

Grandma Crawford

Maple Syrup Time
in the Mountains

Bill and his trusty chainsaw

Re-siding the Parsonage

Christmas Caroling

Dollie and Mari
at the Church

Grace Baptist Church

VBS Parade

Children's Ministries

Billy, Jeff, and Johnny

An Endless Mountain Family

Overflow Sunday School Class

CHAPTER 10

Friends and Fellowship

*A man that hath friends must show himself friendly; and there is
a friend who sticketh closer than a brother. Proverbs 18:24*

The wind continued to howl through the cracks in the parsonage walls, the temperature continued to drop—sometimes to below zero—and we continued to shiver while Bill went into the woods weekly to chop more wood. Often, because he had to borrow tractors from friends, he had to help them spread manure or unload their wood before he could use the tractor.

The mountain weather was not simply "a social invention to facilitate small talk." It was a frightful beast, dominating all activity, schedules, and plans. Only those foolish enough to "tough it out" bothered to set agendas without first checking with the meteorologist. This being our first winter in the Endless Mountains, we were among those who didn't have enough sense to consider the weather when planning our Valentine parties and spring activities.

Because Bill had been asked to speak for the couples' party at a church in Sayre February 13, we decided to have our own Valentine's banquet a week early, on February 6. Since all the church banquets were held in the parsonage living room, I was automatically volunteered as official hostess.

81

I cooked and baked and cleaned all week, preparing for the event, while Bill and his chain saw were busy in the woods. Now, I'm not a bad cook, but my cooking did cure our dog from begging at the table. I worked for hours trying to bake a heart-shaped cake and wound up with a mess—artistic culinary skill obviously is not one of my talents. So I broke up the floury mess, layered it with my raspberry jam into fancy glasses, and voila! I had a lovely parfait dessert.

The weatherman decided to cooperate, and we woke Saturday morning to a beautiful sunny day, 50 degrees that felt like spring. With a rare spurt of energy, I got everything ready for the party in the morning, planning to rest a little before party time. By then, I was really feeling sick and needed to lie down to keep the nausea under control.

Sam Crane had called early that morning, volunteering himself and his boys to help Bill get some wood, "seeing's as how it's such a beautiful day." About 1 o'clock, just as I was getting to rest, the front door opened and in tromped four muddy, dirty Crane boys, plus Billy who was muddier and dirtier than they were. Their mom wasn't home, and my gregarious husband invited them all over for lunch!

Apparently he had forgotten that our cupboards were completely bare except for the party food. I saw no choice but to serve that for lunch. Two hours and a wrecked house later, I had to start all over again. I frantically changed my menu plan and made a quick rush down to Kennedy's for supplies. Less than five minutes before party time, I fell into a chair exhausted and pasted on my best hostess smile, hoping the smile and its owner would last through the evening.

As I commiserated with Mom in my weekly letter, I told her, *"You have no idea what life in a parsonage can be like until you've actually lived in one! We got a whole garage full of good, seasoned wood out of it, so I'm sure it was worth it. And Bill also got a whole day of talking to Sam, which is really important."*

Life in our parsonage was anything but dull. Not only did ours serve as the church fellowship hall, it became a bed and breakfast for many visitors. The assortment of people who slept in our beds that spring included missionaries from Ireland, Liberia, and Rhodesia; RHMA missionaries; homeless teens; visiting relatives; a writer from *Redbook* magazine; even a representative of the American Heart Association who came to check on Bill's health.

We also had frequent fellowship with other RHMA missionaries, who were serving at places like Windham Summit, Bumpville, Jersey Mills, and Oregon Hill. Because our mission stations were so widely spread out, and we happened to have a big house and live more or less in the middle of everyone, our house became the monthly meeting place for the missionaries and their families. Often, some of them spent the night, and we'd have missionaries and kids sprawled all over the house.

Two of our most memorable visitors were new RHMA evangelists, Ken Hanna and Duane Merritt. Recent graduates of Moody Bible Institute, they were traveling in youth evangelism on rural fields. Sponsored by the RHMA, the two were great Bible teachers and musicians who presented fantastic programs. The night before our Valentine party, we took 31 teens down to Franklindale for a youth rally Ken and Duane were leading. Nate and Marge Blow, good friends who didn't attend our church, offered to drive their new Ford bus, which greatly eased the "sardine syndrome" we usually had when packing kids into our tiny car.

News of the impending "hootenanny" spread fast, and our phone rang constantly after school that evening, everybody wanting to be picked up for the fun. Kids we had never heard of invited themselves. We weren't sure they knew this particular "hootenanny" was a Christian one, but whatever their reasons for coming with us, we saw it as a great opportunity for them to hear the Gospel. When it became evident even the Blows' van wouldn't haul all the kids, we managed to enlist three more cars and drivers.

Bill cut wood all afternoon, first for a neighbor and then for us. Early in the evening, he drove over to the Wilcoxes' to help George with chores so they could get done in time to drive a load of kids. While looking forward to the fun evening and praying that many of the kids would get saved, I had a nagging worry. Bill had awakened that morning feeling terrible. His heart was acting up again, his blood pressure was alarmingly high, and he had awful headaches. As we were changing clothes for the evening outing, I noticed his breathing was labored and he seemed winded. I thought back over his exhausting day of getting wood, doing farm chores, and now another late night of ministry. God, how long can he do this? I wondered.

I also worried about my own health. I had run out of nausea pills again and wouldn't be able to get more until our mission check arrived—hopefully on Monday. Grabbing my ever-present barf bag and saltines, I joined my weary country parson and headed for the hootenanny.

We all enjoyed the service in Franklindale so much, we promptly invited the evangelists to do an entire week of meetings at our church. A couple of weeks later, they pulled up to the parsonage in a '57 Chevy, loaded down with books, assorted musical instruments, and luggage. That began a week to be remembered! We stayed up night after night till the proverbial "wee hours of the morning," talking and sharing the goodness of God. Billy and Mari were delighted as the guys taught them the secrets of their magic tricks, which became the foundation of Billy's youth ministries years later. Some of Ken and Duane's hilarious skits also wound their way into our family's camp ministry repertoire years later.

Our people enjoyed the evangelists as much as we did. Those boys really packed in the crowds. By Friday night, every seat in the church was taken, with some folks standing in the back and others piled on laps. We broke all attendance records, but the most excitement came when six young people dedicated their lives to Christian service and another teen accepted Christ.

By this time, the snow had returned with a vengeance. Puny and Bill spent many long hours hauling people to church, slipping and sliding on the icy roads, putting on chains, taking off chains—the usual winter driving routine. God rewarded Bill's faithfulness by prompting someone to send us enough money for an entire ton of coal. Then a big lumber truck came up and dumped a load of sawed slab wood in our garage, compliments of an anonymous donor. The unexpected fuel supply was truly a blessing as Bill's blood pressure was often as high as 280. His heart specialist told him he wouldn't survive any more wood cutting and carrying.

During that hectic week of meetings, we also had another houseguest. A freelance writer was sent out by *Redbook* to write an article on us. She spent part of three days filling up one notebook after another with all sorts of little gems of information about us Midwestern Misfits in the mountains. A medical writer, she became concerned about Bill's heart problems, especially about his high drug and doctor bills. She contacted a friend of hers at the National Heart Association, who in turn sent out an area representative.

The representative gave us all sorts of information on heart disease, diet, and how to get some of Bill's heart drugs at cost. She also offered the hope that the Heart Association might be able to help with some of our past medical expenses from Mayo and Guthrie Clinics.

The writer didn't leave Billy and Mari out of her thoughtfulness, either. Her sister was a children's book writer, who sent a number of books for the kids. They really "strutted their stuff" at school, showing off their autographed copies of the latest books being touted by the Scholastics Book Club.

God was so good, and it was easy to see His hand in all of this. Things began to look up again, even on the financial front. The night janitor at the school became ill, and they asked Bill if he'd come in and keep the fires going all night. They offered to pay him $8 a night and said they may need him for several weeks. It worked out well, as he could sleep during the day at our house and study at night while he was tending the school fires. He stoked our fire before he left each evening, because I still hadn't learned how to keep it going. Fortunately, the weather continued to warm up; the horrible drafty winds had possibly died down for the season.

When *Redbook* decided not to use our story (apparently we were too evangelical for them), the editor promised us a $500 kill fee. I immediately began shopping for my long-desired washer and dryer. Maynard Mathewson had a man in his church who was a GE dealer who offered to get us a set at his cost. The model we chose was $254, just over half of our *Redbook* money. And just in time for the loads of diapers I would soon be washing! However, we couldn't place the order until we actually had the check in hand, which didn't happen for a number of months.

Meanwhile, I continued struggling with the Maytag wringer in the bathroom, but at least I had hope that it was only a temporary arrangement. It's amazing what a little bit of hope can do for one's attitude!

Life became a relentless round of visiting, Bible Clubs, Scout activities, youth parties and rallies, mixed in with the ever-present nausea. One day in late March, I had rushed from my Milan Bible Club to East Smithfield for a Scout leaders' meeting. While sitting in the Fletchers' kitchen, we heard a sickening crash—some guy had rammed into Puny, tearing off the back bumper. By time we exchanged insurance cards and settled things, it was way past time to rush home to pick up Bill for prayer meeting.

Knowing there was no time to waste, I parked Puny in the drive, Mari climbed into the back seat, and I ran into the house to get Bill and Billy. They hadn't come out when I honked. As I approached the front door, I saw Bill on the phone motioning frantically to me. I turned and looked, just in time to see Puny rolling rapidly down our steep drive, with Mari screaming hysterically from the back seat.

Running as fast as I could in my late-pregnancy athleticism, I caught the door handle but couldn't pull it open with the car going so fast. When it finally came open, I flung myself across the front seat, grabbing the brake with my hand, just before it rammed into the tree. About the same time, Billy jerked the other door opened and turned the wheel. Puny halted to a stop, stuck in mud up to his hubcaps.

I got some badly bent fingers, an awfully sore stomach, and a pulled ligament in my pelvis area, not to mention a case of badly jittered nerves out of the ordeal. Mari emerged scratchless but quite shaken up.

By time we got Puny stopped, Bill had hung up the phone and come down to the end of the drive. The phone call was long distance from the State Department of Rehabilitation, which was making arrangements to pay some of his medical bills. Bill was so involved in the call, he didn't see what the rest of us were up to. By then, because it was well past church time, Lee and Levia Burlingame came to check on us. They drove us to church and then came back with us after the service to try to get Puny out of the mud. Since no amount of pulling and tugging could release the car, we decided to call it a night and go to bed.

But a half hour later, Lee drove up on Stub's tractor and pulled Puny out. On their way home, Levia had worried that I might go into labor after my ordeal, and they didn't want us to be without a car all night. They also brought a bag of candy and some potato chips for Billy to thank him for helping us so much with the coal and ashes while his daddy was sick. Every time Satan sent an ordeal around to discourage us, God "one-upped" him by sending along special encouragement from our friends and neighbors.

The accident didn't precipitate labor, but it did put me down for a while. The torn ligament made walking extremely painful, and the doctors wanted to make sure the baby wasn't injured. One of the area pastors bragged up my writing ability at a pastors' fellowship about that time, and soon I was inundated with writing projects—"since I was laid up anyway." They asked me to write the Penn-York Association's quiz questions and voted Bill in as secretary of the association, "because Dollie is such a gifted writer, she can handle all our correspondence." Huh?

Other writing assignments piled in—radio scripts for Light for the Valley, tracts for the local Christian bookstore, even some paying assignments from Christian publishers and Sunday School papers. God used my down time productively, but it meant Bill had to take on more of the housekeeping and cooking chores. Taking into account all the church dinners and friends we hosted, that in itself was a full-time job.

By late April, I was back on my feet, just in time to host a group of RHMA missionaries who were gathering at our place for the showing of RHMA's new film "Open Doors." My last piano student left at 5:30, giving me just enough time to get dinner on the table for our guests, rush off to church for the meeting, and rush back home to get beds ready for those who needed to stay overnight.

Three days later, we hosted the Mother and Daughter banquet in our living room, meaning we shoved all our furniture into the bedrooms to make room for tables for thirty-six guests. Weeks like that were not covered in any of the pastors' wives seminars I had attended. Nor did the seminars teach us what to do with a pastor husband who was "addicted to hospitality." Bill, whose family was deeply rooted in the traditions of Southern hospitality, took seriously Paul's qualifications for church leaders, especially the one about "given to hospitality." He never passed up an opportunity to invite someone over for a meal or to spend the night, confident I could pull something out of my bag of tricks to feed them.

William Wordsworth described hospitality as "a genial hearth, a hospitable board, and a refined rusticity." I don't know how refined we were, but anyone putting in for a night at our house sure got the genial part of it.

Wit-n-Wisdom: When are houses like books? When they have stories in them.

CHAPTER 11

Babies and Blessings

*Children are an heritage of the Lord ... happy is the man
that has his quiver full of them. Psalm 127:3, 5*

The obstetrician planned to induce labor the end of
April, and Mom and my sister Helen planned to
come out to help. Bill invited them, insisting that he
needed Mom Crawford there to replace me on the piano bench, teach,
and lead the ladies' ministry. Helen would handle the housework
and laundry chores. He was to meet their train in Waverly, New
York, at 3 a.m. the night my labor was to be induced.

They arrived, worn out from the eighteen-hour long train ride,
fully expecting to be greeted with news of the baby. Instead, I was
there to meet them. I had come down with a bad strep infection,
and Dr. Corner sent me home from the hospital. "We'll just have to
wait until he decides to come naturally," he explained. "It's much too
dangerous to induce labor when you're already so ill."

So we waited. And waited. And waited. The last week of April
came and went. Then May passed off the calendar. Mom kept
assuring me, "When the apple is ripe, it'll fall." But I got very tired
of the interminable waiting. Helen got tired of waiting, too, and
tired of being gone from her own husband and family so long. She
got her wish to go home in a way none of us could have expected.

89

We received a phone call in the middle of the night from my youngest sister, Elsa. The connection was very bad—we could hear her, but she couldn't hear us. Unable to get a decent connection on our mountain phone, we drove into East Smithfield and located a public phone booth on top the hill and called Elsa back. She frantically told us that her four-year-old daughter had her leg amputated in a mower accident that day. Infection had set in and little Kelly was near death.

Mom was so torn, with two of her daughters desperately needing her at the same time. Together, we all made the decision that Helen would return home to be with Elsa and her family and Mom would stay with me in Pennsylvania until the baby came. She kept close tabs on the granddaughter in Illinois. I'm sure it was Mom's prayers that pulled Kelly through the dreadful ordeal.

The next day we made another early morning trip to the Waverly station to start Helen on a solo trip back to Illinois, while Mom stayed at the parsonage so Billy and Mari wouldn't have to get dragged out of bed so early.

Mom Crawford was one of our greatest blessings from the day we had answered God's call to become missionaries. She was one of our most faithful prayer warriors and often enlisted others to pray. Widowed several years earlier, she was organist, Bible teacher, and camp director at her church. She also served as chairman of the RHMA's Ladies' Auxiliary, a group that mailed all of the monthly missionary letters, helped with conference meals, and pitched in whenever volunteers were needed.

I felt guilty pulling Mom from all her duties, but Bill was more philosophical. "Dollie needs you more right now than the RHMA and Rev. Rupp do," he insisted, referring to her minister. He was right. During the month of waiting for the baby, she took over some of my clubs, played for services, and led the ladies' missionary group. And boy, did she lead!

Women who hadn't called on anyone in years offered to go with her. She soon had those ladies driving all over the area, visiting the sick, taking casseroles to the needy, sewing quilts. They even found some plaster plaque molds and started casting plaques for VBS handcrafts. They cut out my Life of Christ flannelgraph figures for the next semester's Bible Clubs. I think they were surprised and pleased to see how much they could accomplish when they set their minds to it; they just needed a spurt of enthusiasm and encouragement from someone like Mom.

Meanwhile, the Lord continued to pour out blessings on us, preparing for the arrival of Farley Number Three. Chillicothe Bible Church sent pajamas, not only for the expected baby, but for Mari and Billy as well. A church in Danbury, Connecticut, shipped us four large boxes of baby things, and it seemed everybody we knew decided to have a baby shower for us. The RHMA fellowship group had a shower for us at our house, the church ladies hosted another one, my Girl Scouts outdid themselves with gifts for the baby, and the area pastors' fellowship had yet another shower. Many of our supporters sent gifts. We were afraid we'd have to move out of the parsonage to make room for the baby and all his gifts!

I realized we had far more baby items than we could possibly use and asked God how He wanted me to handle it. They had been generously given to us as gifts, and I certainly didn't want to wound anyone's feelings by giving the gift away. God directed us to a nearby tenant farmer and his family, who were on welfare because the husband had had polio and couldn't work. They had just had a new baby and had no baby things at all. I presented the problem to our ladies and "just happened" to mention that I had far more than we needed. Bless their hearts, they picked up on my hint, and offered, "Why don't we go through all the things you have and pick some out for the Smiths?" We spent a delightful afternoon having a "reverse" baby shower, selecting duplicates and extras, rewrapping them, and then taking them over to the delighted couple.

While I had plenty of baby blankets to share, I kept those I especially treasured—the baby quilts and comforters lovingly handcrafted by our friends around the country. An elderly blind lady painstakingly made a soft, cuddly quilt, one that Jeff loved for years as his special security blankie. He became so attached to that thing, I was afraid he would even take it to football camp. We treated a couple of the other quilts as family heirlooms and much later passed them down to grandkids, along with the stories of the people who had made them, to be treasured and remembered.

It was the season for babies in the Endless Mountains. George and Mary had already had their little girl, Lisa, a darling baby who made me eager to get my own out of the "oven." Elsie Crane and Marge Decker also were expecting, as was our home church pastor's wife. Several others in our neck of the woods had already had baby girls, and Bill began to worry that God was only handing out girls. I tried to encourage him, "If we have a boy, he'll be outnumbered by all these girls. If ours is a girl, think of all the playmates she'll have."

He wasn't buying my logic, certain that the baby in my womb was a little boy who would grow up to be a football player. The potential football player kicked in big time on June 5. Rev. Grant and Joy Rice, who had been instrumental in our decision to serve the Lord full-time, surprised us that afternoon by "dropping in" all the way from Monroe, Wisconsin. They had been at a conference out east somewhere and decided we weren't that far off their route. What a thrill!

While Mom, Joy, and I were cooking supper, I nearly doubled over in pain. Thinking it was "The Thumper" (our pet name for the baby) just doing his thing, I continued to set the table and get things ready for our guests. Bill and Mom hovered over me, begging me to head for the hospital, which was at least forty-five minutes away. When the pains grew harder and quicker, I relented. We grabbed my bag and headed up the valley, only to get behind a U-Haul that was crawling along. "I thought I'd never have to tangle with a U-Haul again!" Bill grumbled.

We both felt sure Bill was going to be delivering a baby en route, but we made it to the hospital, just minutes before Jeff poked his head out for his first look at the world. We had left home around 7:00, and Jeff's birth was recorded at 7:53 p.m., meaning Bill did some pretty swift driving, even with that U-Haul in front of us.

Despite all my nausea and weight loss, Jeff was extremely healthy, weighing in at eight pounds, ten ounces—nearly nine pounds of baby! Of course, he looked just like his daddy, who was almost giddy with jubilation. So giddy, in fact, we didn't think he was in any shape to preach the next morning. With perfect timing, God not only sent the Rices to encourage us, but Grant served as extra-special pulpit supply the next morning, and our people got to enjoy a wonderful guest speaker.

We drove Mom up to the train station in Waverly a week or so later to get her back to Illinois in time for her VBS and camp ministries. How I missed her! Dirty diapers piled up and the house was a disaster area waiting to happen, while I tried to adjust hormones and got very little sleep. Before Mom left, she had taken us to the auction house and bought a recliner for Bill, which helped greatly with his nightly breathing problems. He spent the nights in the recliner, and I didn't bother to climb the stairs to our bedroom, preferring to sleep on the couch to tend the baby.

Soon after Jeff was born, one of our ladies received bad news of a close family member back in Connecticut. Her husband planned to drive her there and return immediately. Because he couldn't make such a long drive without sleep, he asked Bill to accompany him and do half the driving. Bill didn't really want to go and leave me alone with the kids. I didn't really want him to go either, considering the state of his health and his extreme fatigue. But he felt God wanted him to help out, so they left at noon, drove all night, and returned home about 7 a.m., exhausted.

In the meantime, Barbie decided she didn't want me to be alone, and "besides," she said, "I need some time to talk with you." So I had a sleepover guest and counseled with her all night. Another of our church families brought hot dogs up for supper and stayed the evening, figuring I'd be lonesome with Bill gone. Ungrateful wretch that I am, I would have enjoyed getting good and lonesome for about 24 hours!

The Longeneckers came out shortly after that, and the area missionaries all came to our house to see them. All the guests, on top of a new baby, were too much. In a letter to Mom, I complained about my plight:

> *Had our fellow missionaries here all day Thursday; they stayed until late that night, visiting with the Longeneckers, and letting their kids run wild. Talk about nervous exhaustion! When the last car finally pulled out of the drive, I just went to pieces—what a day! I couldn't even feed Jeff that night and had to give him Similac for the first time.*
>
> *One of their babies had diarrhea and kept messing all over the place, then crawling around on Jeff's baby things, even messing all over his new high chair. The toddlers kept poking at him and pulling his ears. I tried putting him in Mari's room and closing the door, but the only thing that accomplished was that I couldn't see what they were doing to him.*
>
> *So I sat and held him most of the day, with everyone accusing me of spoiling him. Could hardly tell 'em I was protecting him, not spoiling him!!*

The next week was VBS and then it was time to take the kids up to New York for camp. With almost no let-up in activity, Bill and I were just plumb exhausted. I went into a severe bout of postpartum depression and Bill was very sick, unable to keep food down. I think we were both worn out physically, yet none of our church folks even guessed we were ill. God always granted us enough "steam" to accomplish the task at hand before we utterly collapsed at home.

VBS attendance was down from the previous year, with only sixty-three kids registered. We had apparently picked a bad time, right in the midst of haying season. Then, too, President Johnson's anti-poverty program started a special summer session at school for all the welfare kids, feeding them and taking them on field trips, drastically cutting into our VBS attendance. Despite all that, ten kids made decisions to accept Christ, and two others dedicated their lives to Him.

Continuing to complain to Mom, I listed the day's frantic activities:

> *It's after 11, and I finally got everybody tucked in, more or less. Sure hope we get some sleep tonight—was awake with Bill all last night and haven't gotten to bed before midnight for weeks. Have a load of dishes to do yet tonight. I was still hanging up diapers at 7 (pm, unfortunately!), and we didn't get supper till 9 o'clock. It was like Grand Central Station here.*

> *Saturday, we drove up to camp to pick up Billy and Joanie, getting home just in time to clean the church for the Penn-York Youth Rally, which turned out real good! Then church today, trying to get things in order here at the house for company for supper, and cleaning the church again for the program. And so goes the daily life of your Endless Mountain missionaries!*

Billy enjoyed camp, but got his first lesson in the ways of women, much to his chagrin. He got stood up for his first "date," a pastor's daughter who invited him to take her to the camp banquet. When he showed up at her cabin, all spruced up and ready to party, Sherry left him cooling his nine-year-old heels for about five minutes, then sent another girl out to tell him she'd changed her mind. Heartbreak!

About that same time, both kids got an early lesson in the birds and the bees. We went with the Blows to their cabin way back in the woods on Armenia Mountain, a remote place of indescribable peace and tranquility. Billy, Mari, and the Blows' children scurried off down the woodland path, eager to fill their buckets with huckleberries. We warned them to stay on the path, but on their way back to the cabin they saw another path leading out into a beautiful meadow and decided to take a sidetrack.

Seeing a car and a truck parked in the meadow, both with their doors wide open, the kids went to investigate. This was during the age of innocence, long before the sexual revolution hit the country, and when they saw a man and woman lying in the back seat, both sans clothes, they panicked and hit the trail. Berries flew from their buckets as they tried to outrun the car, which was now coming down the trail toward them. They hid in the bushes, breathless and terrified, until the car driver gave up looking for them and left.

Billy was selected to come into the cabin and explain why they were so late getting back. After he had calmed down, I took him aside and began to explain the facts of life. I don't know what I said to him, but when he went back outside, he told the others, "Mom says we shouldn't be afraid. They were just making babies."

An added perk of living in the mountains was the opportunity to enjoy the old-fashioned pleasures of village life. The weekend of the huckleberry fiasco, Mari rode the Brownie float in the East Smithfield Fourth of July parade, then we all went to our friends' farm along the Susquehanna River for a traditional holiday picnic. That evening, we invited some of our fellow missionaries for supper before going to the fireworks.

John Adams said the Fourth of July should be celebrated "with pomp and parade, with shews, games, sports, guns, bells, bonfires, and illuminations from one end of this continent to the other." East Smithfield took Adams at his word, pulling out all the stops to celebrate America's birthday. The parade, complete with fife and drums corps and dozens of floats, wound through town and around the Village Green, led by valiant patriots in Revolutionary War regalia. Modern airmen parachuted onto the green in a dazzling display of good aim.

Following an ice cream social on the lawn of the Federated Church, we enjoyed fire truck rides, dunk tanks, and all sorts of small town festivities before heading for our picnic. The piece de la resistance, however, was the fireworks show that began after dark. Everyone assembled around the mountains surrounding the town, each clan having its own favorite spot. Cars and pickup trucks lined the hillsides; their occupants climbed on the hoods or roofs for a better view of the fireworks battle. Old-timers walked along, flashing lights in faces to see who was there, sharing apple pie and other goodies from car to car, sort of like today's tailgate parties. I think there was even a little Endless Mountain moonshine shared along the route.

The American Legion and the VFW shot their fireworks in a battle from opposing mountains, while the valleys reverberated with the lingering echoes of that great war for independence. Enjoying this spectacle and the accompanying hospitality, we could almost feel the presence of the original soldiers who had fought on these same mountains nearly 200 years earlier. Knowing some of them lay beneath tombstones just down the road from our house made us appreciate even more the great country they had fought to secure for us.

Reliving history wasn't the only blessing God had in store for our kids. Dad Farley had been especially vocal about our pulling Mari and Billy out of "good schools to take them to some backwoods area where they won't get a good education." How wrong he was! Our elementary school in East Smithfield was staffed with loving, caring teachers, and though they were a bit behind Illinois schools in some areas, they were "far enough behind to be ahead" where it counted.

Phonics, basic values, and traditional lessons laid a great foundation for our kids, while their counterparts back in Illinois were being exposed to "modern methods" and experiments in all sorts of "educational" techniques. The country, especially the educational system, was in the throes of the wild '60s. Since we didn't have television and couldn't afford the weekly newspaper, we virtually escaped that wild time in American history. Our '60s generation kids grew up without being exposed to the drugs, free love, and rebellion that infected an entire generation. Tucked away in the Endless Mountains, they enjoyed a wonderful childhood, protected by God Himself.

They learned the fine art of self-entertainment, as well. Instead of relying on television and movies, they learned to create their own games, along with a host of parlor games that didn't require a trip to a toy store. Most evenings, and every church party, offered the old-fashioned games our parents and grandparents had played. Winkum, upset the fruit basket, poor kitty, fur feather fin, when the spirit moves, hangman, charades, kick the can, sardines, spoons—you name it, the kids learned to play it.

Billy and Mari enjoyed growing up in the Endless Mountains. In addition to huckleberrying, they often got to ride on hay wagons, swim in rocky pools in the mountain streams, and hike spectacular mountain trails. Fun trips with the youth group let them explore wonderful places like the Grand Canyon of Pennsylvania and Watkins Glen. An invitation from fellow missionaries took them to an insider's look at how the Amish lived and worked. And what child wouldn't enjoy shopping at Kennedy's Market, a grocery-cum-hardware store where for a nickel you could buy fresh-made maple sugar candy?

Billy's favorite thing was getting to go maple sugarin' with his dad and some of the men from the church. These all-night events usually featured wiener roasts while waiting for the sap to boil down, and Billy discovered that eggs boiled in the sap were delightful eating. He bonded with the men, who became his life-long heroes. Men like George Wilcox, who showed him that married guys could be zany and have lots of fun, and Stub Wittie, whose hardtack life demonstrated how hard work could be made fun and satisfying.

When we answered God's call to go to the mountains to feed His sheep, most of our friends and family thought we were crazy—

"giving up" great careers, a nice home, good paychecks, and many friends. But we didn't give up anything that God didn't replace a hundredfold. Yes, there were challenges and lessons of faith to learn. As a result, our move to Pennsylvania changed our lives forever, and the things we learned there are still being carried forward from generation to generation.

Wit-n-Wisdom: There is so much to teach, and the time goes so fast— Erma Bombeck

CHAPTER 12

Midwest Moxie Vs. Mountain Mellow

*Whosoever will come after me, let him deny himself, and
take up his cross, and follow me. Mark 8:35*

"We can't possibly take the whole summer off to go on
deputation," we argued. "Our people need us too
much, and Dollie's still so sick from Jeff's birth."

Rev. Longenecker was patient but persistent. "Your support is
much too low, and Bill's health is much too poor for him to continue
working like this. If you can't go for the entire summer, at least plan
on taking a month or six weeks."

Fighting postpartum depression, an infection of the uterus and
bladder, plus a general rundown anemic condition, I directed VBS
and continued plowing through laundry, gardening, canning—all
the things I thought a good pastor's wife must do. The doctor decided
to cauterize my uterus to stop the heavy bleeding, then gave me
prescriptions for the bladder infection and shots for the anemia.

Figuring I was as healthy as I was going to get, and knowing
that Rev. Longenecker's advice was sound, we prepared to go back
to the Midwest for the entire month of August, scheduling services

at as many churches as we could fit into our days. And what a trip! We had such a great time that Bill told Rev. Longenecker we'd like to be permanent missionaries on furlough.

We were scheduled for breakfast, lunch, and dinner every day, with others inviting us for late-night refreshments when they learned our days were filled up. Treated like royalty everywhere we went, it would have been easy to slip into a "celebrity mentality" and think we were worthy of all that praise. We knew better, of course, and fought the temptation to think of ourselves "more highly than we ought to think."

However, we did allow ourselves to slip into an even more dangerous mentality, comparing our country church and its people with the well-equipped, beautiful sanctuaries and industrious leaders of our supporting churches. "If only we had deacons and leaders like that!" we often commiserated to each other. "Or how would it be to have Sunday School teachers who decorate their rooms and make them so inviting for the kids?" we mused.

Loaded with ideas and equipment (generous gifts from our friends), we returned to Pennsylvania rarin' to go. We would get things fired up and running right in the mountains! By "right," of course, we meant our Midwest way of doing things.

Renewed in body, soul, and spirit, and glowing with enthusiasm to tackle the work with vim, vigor, and vitality, we headed up Mill Road toward the parsonage, eager to unload our treasures and get busy. At first glance, we thought our house had been the victim of a capricious storm—everything about our "feudal castle" on the hilltop looked different.

The dead pear tree and old mulberry were both gone, the rotten siding was torn off the front of the house, roof shingles were piled up on the ground. Pulling into our drive, we saw the wood from the dead trees was neatly stacked in the garage. Someone had torn off the ancient weather-beaten siding, preparing the front to be replaced with insulation, tarpaper, and lovely white clapboards.

As we drew closer to the "wreckage," we noticed new paint on the doors and trim. Inside, an even greater shock greeted us, a complete redo! Gorgeous, country wallpaper in the living room; gleaming, freshly painted woodwork; ceilings scraped, repaired, and repainted; cabinets cleaned and stocked with groceries; a freezer full of vegetables for the winter; a new cabinet over the stove; even my bushels of ironing had been done. Someone had cleaned all the venetian blinds, scrubbed our dinette set, used "Dip-it" on all our dishes, and polished the place till it shone. It literally looked like the magazine pictures of the lovely farmhouses I had always coveted.

After our initial shock, Bill called Stub, our head deacon, and jokingly asked, "How soon do we have to move out to make room for the new preacher?" As soon as the unofficial grapevine carried the news that "The Farleys are home!" folks started dropping by. We heard story after story of how they had worked together, some of the funny things that had happened, and what a great time they had had working on our surprise. It sounded like so much fun, we were sorry we missed it all.

Apparently, everything was still in a total shambles that weekend, and Stub, in his usual prankster way, about gave the ladies heart failure, telling them we had changed our plans and were coming home a day early.

They were all so thrilled with their surprise for us, they had to show us everything. Like little kids, we ran from room to room, taking in all the changes and admiring their handiwork. In the excitement, one of the fellows asked, "Have you seen the church yet?"

Late as it was, we all hustled down to the church to admire the remodeled and redecorated entry.

We fell into bed that night, exhausted but bubbling over with thankfulness and excitement. With all our new ideas coupled with such wonderful, energetic people, Grace Baptist Church would once again be the lighthouse God intended it to be.

The following Friday was our tenth wedding anniversary. Mabel Wilcox invited herself for supper, then later called and asked if she could bring her daughter, Esther Kitchen, over too. When they both came in, dressed "to kill," we sort of expected their entire family was planning to surprise us. But they both were so casual at supper and seemed in no hurry to get things cleared up, we decided they weren't trying to pull anything on us after all.

About 8:15 a string of cars pulled in, horns blaring, pans crashing. It seemed everybody in the area was there to "horn" us for our anniversary. They gave us lovely gifts to complement our new décor, and we all had a marvelous time of fun and fellowship.

They also got us a couple loads of bulk ash logs and sat up a tractor and buzz saw to cut the wood to the right size without too much hard work for Bill. A gift from Illinois allowed us to purchase two tons of coal, and the new insulation and siding on the parsonage would help keep the house warmer. With our heating fuel provided, I felt free to use the money I'd saved from my piano students and writing to get my long-desired automatic washer. The REDBOOK money I'd planned to use never did come through, so I had spent many more months bending over the old wringer than we anticipated. I don't think I've ever welcomed anything more than that beautiful Westinghouse automatic in my bathroom!

Ah, yes, it was going to be a great year, and we were going to accomplish great and mighty things for God!

We hadn't begun to settle down from all our blessings when the problems began rolling in. Bill drove up to visit one of our men who was in an Elmira hospital. Before he got home, a friend called to tell us her baby was having emergency surgery for a strangulated hernia. I managed to call Bill before he left Jim's room, and he was able to spend the rest of the day comforting the Deckers. He got home late that evening, just in time to tackle a tougher task.

The church's Missionary Society treasurer sent her books back and had piled the Sunday School treasurer supplies in front of the church. One of the other leadership couples went to see what the problem was and came back with the report that "Bill's preaching was too strong." They especially didn't like his telling them that Sunday School teachers and leaders should attend all services, not just Sunday School.

Discouraged, we discussed the problem with our field director, who counseled us it would be good to "weed out the dead wood" who weren't doing their jobs and that this might be God's way of making the church stronger. Coupled with our desire for Grace Baptist to be more like our Midwestern Bible-belt churches, we consoled ourselves by agreeing with him.

The next night, Bill picked up one of the other deacons to go with him to call on the offended family. He was met by a badly shaking, browbeaten man. The deacon came out to the car and said he had "talked things over with his wife." They agreed that if the Witties left, they were leaving too.

God gave Bill the grace to answer the deacon's accusations tactfully. Bill pointed out that just the previous night, they both had been in total agreement about the situation. "What happened between then and now to change your mind so completely?" he asked.

The deacon hung his head and admitted, "My wife. She says you really are trying to run the church." He refused to call on the other family with Bill, but he confessed he didn't want to leave the church.

Bill went alone to pray with Stub and Marian and to apologize for offending them. To his surprise, they said they were behind his ministry all the way and had no intention of leaving the church. She had been ill and didn't want to continue all her jobs in light of the problems the other family was causing.

Proverbs 11:13 says, "A gossip goes about spreading rumors, while a trustworthy man tries to quiet them." Bill spent the next month or so trying to put out the gossip fires that were blazing throughout the church community. "He said/she said" rumors were causing all sorts of strife and backbiting. At one point, things got so bad I honestly was afraid to sleep at night because a man had threatened to burn down our house. I poured out all our heartache in a long letter to Mom, detailing many of the accusations and problems.

Bill came in and asked what I was writing, and I replied, "I'm just telling Mom about our troubles."

"Troubles? We haven't any troubles—nothing that won't wash out in the next rain! Let me see what you've written…." he said, reaching for the letter.

My griping and complaining in the letter was so bad that Bill told me to tear up the first seven pages of it! "You've written it out of your system now," he told me. "So there's no need to worry them with such little problems. It's not nearly as bad as you think, and God's going to take care of it."

Little problems? I thought our world was coming to an end! Especially when one of the families began writing letters of complaint to the RHMA office asking that we be removed. Had it only been three months earlier they had given Bill a standing vote of unanimous approval?

Much more patient than me, Bill totally believed in the concept of "heaping coals of fire." He continued to knock himself out helping his detractors, driving them on errands, pulling their vehicles out of snowdrifts, even spending an entire night in the bitter cold helping to search for a lost billfold. He continued to pray for them and suggested that I should pray for them too. "I find it hard to honestly pray anything but 'get rid of them' Lord!" was my immature reply. Like David of old, I just wanted God to "cast my enemies in a pit!"

Ernie Gonzales, the RHMA field secretary, came for a visit and brought along the letters of complaint, plus Rev. Longenecker's replies, which were masterpieces of tact and truth. As usual when anyone came from the home office, we hosted all the area RHMA missionaries at our house. What a crowd! As we recruited more and more workers in our area, our fellowship circle grew almost beyond the bounds of our house, big as it was. We were so crowded around our tables, we could barely bend our elbows enough to get food in our mouths. Someone said we should learn from that and feed each other with one hand tied behind our back!

The group left just in time for us to head to our church quarterly business meeting, where Ernie hoped to bring order to the chaos. My being so tired from entertaining guests all day didn't help my

nervous jitters any, and Bill was uptight about the whole ordeal—
not good for his already high blood pressure and my still-lingering
postpartum depression.

One of the families began by "blowing off steam" right at
the beginning of the meeting, and the tension in the room fairly
crackled. Stub and George, bless their hearts, began quipping and
joking around, which helped relax the situation. Ernie's presence also
helped settle people down, and somehow we got through the tense
evening. Still not satisfied because we weren't "thrown out on our
ear," the primary complainers invited Ernie to their home the next
evening so they could tell him the "whole story."

In our monthly prayer letter, we barely mentioned the problems
we were having but urged our supporters "to pray for us like you've
never prayed before!" And in my weekly complaint letter to Mom,
I moaned, *"I don't know when so many things have gone wrong all at
once like this! I can't sleep at night—I keep casting all my care into God's
hopper, but a few minutes later I've got it all back again chewing on it!"*

To add insult to injury, one of our new families, ones we'd really
come to depend on, stopped by to tell us that if the people "won't
let us move ahead and do things right, we're going to leave." We
were really caught "betwixt and between"—the old-timers who had
been faithful for years, and the newcomers who, like us, wanted to
see faster progress.

An old adage says, "Too soon old; too late schmart!" God finally
got it through our thick skulls what the root of the problem was. The
primary problem-causing family lived in a dilapidated house that was
literally falling apart around them, and when the newcomers had
begun the push to get the parsonage remodeled, they were green with
envy. The parsonage was already much nicer and more modern than
their ancient farmhouse. She was a Bible college graduate and had felt
God's call on her life to missions years earlier and was frustrated that
her life had turned out so differently than what she expected.

To make things worse, she had been a student during the time
when her college was split by denominational differences, among much

rancor and hard feelings. Years later, she continued to hold bitterness and grudges against that denomination. Every time we fellowshipped with area pastors and churches from the group who had been involved in the split, she felt it was an affront against her personally. Her bitterness spilled over onto us, and she accused us of "being too Baptist!" This was all news to us, since, after all, we were pastoring a Baptist church! Having no knowledge of her long-ago wounds, we had continued to aggravate them. Each time we took our youth group to one of their rallies or invited a missionary from that denomination to speak, it "picked the scab" and reopened her wounds.

God also showed us that in our eagerness to push things through with our Midwest Moxie (chutzpah, even!), we were gravitating toward the newcomers who were more like us. In the process, we were trampling all over the feelings and culture of our faithful few. "Somehow, Lord," we prayed, "help us to minister effectively to all our people. Give us grace to slow down and wait on You."

I'd like to say our new awareness solved the problem, but it didn't right away. It did give us a more patient and understanding love for our people and helped us adjust our attitude. Eventually, the offending family seemed to be reconciled to working with us, and church attendance was higher than it had ever been. On Rally Day, we aimed for the record of 70, which had been set in 1956—just before the church suffered a bad split. We hoped and prayed our high attendance wouldn't bring the same fate.

The Sunday School superintendent had made a crazy contraption with which to break the record over Bill's head. Bill tried it on for size and joked about what a dangerous weapon it was. "Boy, who would ever want to hit a poor defenseless preacher with a thing like this?" he asked.

Chet Decker answered drolly from the back, "Someone who doesn't like him very much!" Considering the trouble we'd just gone through with the superintendent's family, everyone thought it was hilarious and just roared with laughter.

To crown the day, one of our teenagers who had accepted Christ the previous week brought his 13-year-old nephew forward to receive

Christ. My eyes were so full of grateful tears, I could barely see to play the piano for the remainder of the invitation.

Even our Wednesday night prayer meetings averaged high attendance, something that had never been done in the history of the church. Our young people's group continued to grow, and we had thirty-four teens for a Halloween party.

But Satan wasn't about to give up without a fight and continued to harass us with financial woes. Our support had been way down, the bills kept piling up, and no money was coming in. Finally, we prayed that if we didn't receive some income soon, Bill was going to go job hunting. He went to the employment office to see about taking a part-time job, but when his cardiologist heard of it, he laid down the law—absolutely NO work. "What are you trying to do, kill yourself?" he thundered. He tried to explain to us that Bill was in much worse shape than he seemed to think he was and warned him to take it easy.

"Taking it easy" wasn't in Bill's vocabulary. Because our diet was back to peanut butter sandwiches again, he decided to try his hand at hunting. His first try was successful; he brought home a couple of wild grouse. I didn't have the slightest idea how to cook them, so I concocted something and called it "wild grouse a la Farley." I learned early on that what I lacked in cooking skills and preparation could be compensated for by creative presentation. Actually, the grouse was delicious, or maybe I was just so sick of peanut butter sandwiches that anything would have tasted good.

The next day, Bill and his trusty rifle brought home two squirrels for the table. It began to look like we had a Nimrod in the family. Grouse, squirrels, deer, and smelt became our steady diet until I sold a story to *Christian Life* magazine for $75 and we could afford to buy domestic meat again.

Wit-n-Wisdom: In this little jingle, there is a lesson true, You belong either to the building or to the wrecking crew.

CHAPTER 13

Juggling the Juggernaut

A merry heart doeth good like a medicine. Proverbs 17:22

Tensions more or less calmed down at church, with us walking a tight rope between the "newbies" and the "oldies," trying to keep everybody happy and on board. Bill continued to heap his coals of fire, loving his distracters and doing for everybody.

And with characters like George and Stub, it was hard not to have fun. They kept us laughing during the most difficult times and usually kept business meetings light-hearted. During Bible sword drills, we often pitted the adults vs. the teens, giving the youth practice for their Quiz Team matches. Stub gave it the old college try, making much ado about trying to find the passage. Inevitably, he'd give up, hold his Bible high in the air, and declare: "That book ain't in my Bible! Somebody done tore it out!"

During quiz practices, both Stub and George would throw in crazy answers, just to get everybody laughing. "Epistles? They're the wives of the apostles!" Or, "Jacob's brother was named See saw." And "See saw sold his copyright for a mess of potash." How we praised God for their silly shenanigans and tomfoolery that helped lighten the tension we were often feeling.

God gave us a merry heart on the home front as well, in the form of our little "Thumper." Jeff kept us laughing through many a dark moment, and we felt he was God's special gift to keep us smiling. I wrote all his antics to both Grandmas back in Illinois to keep them posted on his development. In one letter, I wrote:

> *I bet Jeff is the only four-month old in history who has worn holes in the soles of his baby shoes! I babysit Lisa while Mary works at Kennedy's to pay off their grocery bill, and they bring her walker over. Jeff just kept watching Lisa going all over in it with a puzzled look. Then he pushed off with his feet in his walker and scooted a few inches. He looked down at his feet and tried it again. Then he just squealed with delight because he'd finally figured it out. From that moment on, there was no stopping him … he's all over the house and into everything. One of his favorite tricks is to "drive" into the bathroom and unload the stacked, clean diapers one at a time from his changing table. Then he shakes them out and gives them a gleeful toss.*

One evening Billy got spanked for some trespass, and Jeff cried and cried in sympathy. We all laughed so hard Billy almost stopped crying to laugh with us. When Billy started bawling again, Jeff really wailed, howling up a storm. The bond between the big brother and baby brother became very strong. Billy often harnessed himself up to Jeff's walker and became his "horsy." Jeff looked like a little Roman general in his chariot, laughing with merriment.

The weather had turned frightfully cold, and the wind howled through our house. Even the new front insulation wasn't keeping it out, and we fought to keep the fire going. One morning about 4 a.m. Bill went downstairs to check the stove. He found Billy fully dressed sitting alongside Jeff's crib, the fire going good. Betty Bourne had mentioned at prayer meeting that night about a cradle virus that was killing so many babies with bulbar pneumonia. Billy was so afraid that Jeff would catch it if he got cold that he stayed up all night making sure the fire didn't go out.

All three kids were such a blessing to us that Bill started making noises about wanting to start another one. I said, "Bite your tongue! I'm not hankering to go through another year like this one for a while!" It was, in fact, exactly a year to the day that I first went to the obstetrician that Dr. Corner finally gave me a clean bill of health—a full year of nausea and illness. But, as any mother will agree, the results were worth it.

At our Thanksgiving praise service the night before Thanksgiving, our "splinter" groups laughed and fellowshipped together like old friends, a fact that brought much joy to our battle-weary hearts. We spent Thanksgiving Day in Bumpsville with another RHMA family and enjoyed a relaxing, lazy day, playing games, eating, eating, and eating. Our hosts, Ken and Peggy Buch, didn't like white meat turkey, so she sent all the white meat home with us, so we enjoyed creamed turkey, turkey hash, and turkey gobbledy gook for a few days. God gave us plenty of rest, merriment, and good food to tide us over for the trying days that were just ahead.

Our income plummeted to an all-time low, and the freezer was empty. All the wonderful items our people had pounded us with a couple of months earlier had been used up, due to our extensive entertaining, church suppers, and missionary gatherings at our house. What should have been enough for our family for the entire winter vanished into that land called "hospitality and sharing." Neither Bill nor I could pass up an opportunity to share with someone in need while our own freezer was full, so much of it had gone to help families who were burned out, laid off, or ill.

When we had gone without any meat for more than a week, we were delighted to get a call from one of our church families. "We just butchered our steer," she began, and my taste buds were already salivating at the thought of a steak, or at least a juicy hamburger. "And we found last year's tongue and liver in the bottom of the

113

freezer. We were going to give it to the dogs, but thought maybe you could use it," she continued.

Not even *this year's* tongue and liver! "I wonder if there's a special reward for such generous people in Heaven?" I later complained to Bill. He laughed, and reminded me of the stories we had heard about people sending used tea bags to missionaries. He added his usual optimistic suggestion, "Liver is supposed to be really good for you. Let's call Mom and find out how to cook it."

The Blows brought us a live duck, and I was about ready to add "cotton pickin' duck pluckin'" to my parson's wife resume. We kept Simon in the garage while I reconciled myself to pluckin' and cookin' duck. Finally the day came that we were so hungry for meat, be it fowl or foul, Bill went out to the garage, hatchet in hand, to do the deed.

Billy went ballistic, crying hysterically. "You can't kill Simon! He's my pet!" That's when we learned the wisdom of never giving a name to something you intend to eat. We knew that none of us would be able to swallow a single bite of Simon, so instead of feeding us, he became yet another mouth to feed.

The family who had instigated much of the trouble at church moved to Milan and became managers of a gas station and store there. With them gainfully employed and out of the immediate neighborhood, things quieted down considerably at church. With nicer living quarters and a steady income, their attitude improved considerably as well.

Barbie, the teen who had caused us no end of problems, got married (against our counsel) and moved out of the area about the same time. With one more time-consumer out of the picture, we looked forward to all the free time we would have to build up the church.

We started a Couples' Club with monthly fellowships, usually at someone's house. We had great fun and camaraderie, all of which helped grow church attendance. One night after Thanksgiving, the couples decided to go bowling for our monthly activity, which, of course, was way outside our budget. We didn't say why, but just told them not to count on us that evening. Someone anonymously sent bowling money for us and hired a babysitter. We enjoyed our first real evening "out" in a year and a half, and I "burned up the alleys" with a very high score.

For every discouraging downtime, God always threw in added blessings, so that, on balance, we were actually far ahead in the blessings department. Just when we were down to our last bag of coal, Stub took Bill to get an oil heater for the kitchen. Because Bill's heart was acting up so badly, I was afraid for him to split the big hunks of roots, the only wood left in the garage. We had been buying coal by the bag whenever we had a couple of dollars.

When folks from church dropped in at the parsonage, they always complained about how cold it was and often said, "We really ought to put a furnace in here." But nothing was ever done about it, and when it did come up at a business meeting, the idea was shot down. "We have to get our own wood; the preacher can get his own."

"The preacher" was getting weaker and weaker but kept trying to keep his family warm. Sometimes, when the south wind blew, the wood stove would get red hot and still not send any heat into the room. We usually gravitated toward the new oil heater in the kitchen to warm up, just using enough wood or coal in the living room to keep it above freezing. Sheldon, one of our newer men, came by and split up some of the huge chunks for Bill, then came over on Saturday to get us another load, easing the heat problem for a couple of weeks.

It got so cold, we joked that we had to go up and break the smoke off the chimney and our words came out in ice cubes. On the serious side, we could see our breath inside the house, the eggs congealed on our plates, and I often wrapped Jeff up in a big blanket and just cuddled him close to me to keep him warm. In one of our letters to the home office, we asked if they had any openings for RHMA missionaries in Hawaii.

Despite the cold and foul weather, church attendance stayed high. One Sunday, Bill told the folks, "We've been here nearly a year and a half already. I know some of you are no doubt tired of us by now." He paused, and then added, "As soon as the offerings pick up and you can afford a full-time preacher, the sooner you'll be rid of us!"

That night, the treasurer handed Bill our weekly check, a percentage of the total offering. Smiling, she asked, "Got your bags packed?" It was the largest offering since we'd been there, $73. Our "cut" was $39, not enough for a family to live on, but much more than the two or three dollars we had been accustomed to getting.

We continued to see fruit from previous years. A young couple who had grown up in Riggs, Ken and Gloria Marple, applied to the RHMA and were accepted for a field on the West Coast. They came by Thanksgiving night to tell us all about their trip to the home office and said that Rev. Longenecker used our church as an example and case study for new candidates during orientation.

The Marples held special meetings at our church that weekend along with Gloria's sister who was a musical evangelist. Our little church rocked that weekend, with large crowds enjoying cowbells, glasses, and a lot of foot-stomping, hand-clappin' mountain music. The Marples were the first of several area couples who joined the RHMA, due to what Rev. Longenecker called "our contagious enthusiasm." We were thrilled to see our friends and co-workers catching our burden for rural America.

We also were thrilled to see that our people were taking Bill's messages to heart. He preached on the sin of idleness, and at the next Ladies' Missionary Meeting, we accomplished more than we had in an entire year's worth of meetings. We made two beautiful quilts, four traveling bags for the Dunn children (our missionaries in Rhodesia), six gift boxes for the nursing home. We also bought a waste basket for the church, accepted a range for the church annex, and made a hanging mobile for the new nursery area we were decorating. Topping it off, they voted to spend Friday in Betty Bourne's kitchen making Christmas treats for the kids instead of buying hard candy.

Friday saw Betty's kitchen transformed into Ye Olde Sweet Shoppe, with about a dozen happy women concocting all sorts of delicacies. No one would have believed these were the same women who only a year earlier "couldn't be bothered" to get together and do something for missions. We thanked God for all the good will and merriment and fervently hoped it would last longer than the Christmas season.

Wit-n-Wisdom: Laughter is an affirmation of God's final triumph over the worst that can befall us.

CHAPTER 14

The Best Christmas Pageant Ever

Have you entered into the treasures of the snow? Job 38:22

ill's health was too precarious to even consider driving back to Illinois for our annual family Christmas. We consoled ourselves by keeping even busier than usual, preparing for a spectacular Christmas pageant and celebration with our church family.

Our Scout executives knew someone who owned a costume shop and took us to meet her. The shop owner not only had a fabulous array of nativity costumes, she offered to let us take anything we could use for free. Instead of the usual bathrobe-clad actors with towels for headpieces, our shepherds and Joseph had the real thing, complete with wigs and beards. Our Wise Men were absolutely elegant in their royal regalia, and our King Herod wore a toga-type Roman robe.

Our newly energized ladies put everything they had into the pageant, outdoing themselves with scenery and backdrops. We rehearsed and rehearsed, and were too busy to lament not going home for Christmas.

Every pastor's wife who directs the Christmas pageant knows a simple fact—every kid within miles of the church will show up and want a part in the play. Our Sunday School and youth group attendance

119

swelled dramatically the weeks before Christmas, and I was hard put to decide who would get the choicest parts in the pageant. Then I remembered my own younger days, and the choosing was easy.

"The Best Christmas Pageant Ever," that classic story about the hilarious happenings when a family of unchurched urchins get involved in the church Christmas pageant, could have been written about my family. We weren't unchurched, but our big family of poor country kids definitely qualified us as "urchins."

Dad was on the board of one of those huge mega churches back before mega churches became the norm. There were no simple little Christmas programs for our church—they were full-scale productions, complete with orchestration, drama, and dance. And since my folks were major supporters of the church, my siblings and I were always assured of a part; not big parts mind you, but parts nonetheless.

With our homemade dresses, scuffed shoes, sagging socks, and stringy hair that looked like shredded zucchini, my sisters and I were not the adorable children a fancy church like that would want to parade up front. We usually got relegated to sing in one of the choirs, where a lovely choir robe would cover up our country clothes. And a seat in the back row would hide our manure-stained shoes.

The image-conscious pastor had a darling daughter, who always got to be the Christmas angel, but we all knew Margie was no angel! She might have looked heavenly, but she was one of those inferior people with a superiority complex, always looking down her patrician nose at us country bumpkins.

My brother could send her into a tailspin by wiping his runny nose across the sleeve of his shepherd's robe or by singing loudly in her ear, "Hark the hairy angels sing!" One year, Margie was picked to be the pageant narrator. Standing importantly at the front lectern, she read, "Caesar Augustus sent out a decree that all the world should be taxed...." She lost her place in confusion when Loren loudly whispered, "He must have been a Democrat!"

With those ancient memories to guide me, I knew who to pick for the best parts. The straggliest-haired girl I could find would be Mary, and the rowdiest terror in the Sunday School would be my

Joseph. And the angel? I bypassed the little blonde darlings and chose instead a chubby little girl with dark skin and hair, a girl who never dreamed of playing an angel. Whoever decreed that the heavenly cherubs were all Scandinavian blondes anyway?

Rounding up all the neighborhood unlikelies, I filled out my cast of shepherds and wise men. Even the most unkempt little rascals can look regal swathed in real velvet robes and a wise man's crown. The shepherd's costumes could disguise the grimiest of jeans, and the manure-covered shoes just lended authenticity to the scene.

The pageant was a tremendous success, bringing in the parents of our budding young Thespians, many of whom heard the Christmas story for the first time. We distributed the delightful goodies the ladies had made, then the church folks surprised us with a footstool and end table to match our furniture, plus a desk lamp and $95 to help us get caught up on our bills.

The Witties brought us a basket with fresh hamburger and steaks (no liver or tongue this time!!), and Kennedy's Market gave us a lovely food basket, with lots of fresh fruit. Earlier that week, the Buchs' church in Windham Summit had a food shower for us. It was going to be a great holiday!

Because we were so busy rehearsing for the pageant and having all the church activities, we decided to wait until the week between the pageant and Christmas to do our own shopping for the kids' presents and to lay in the goodies for our holiday dinner. Emptying the piggy bank we planned to use for our shopping trip, we decided to drive the 40 miles to Elmira the next morning, pick up our holiday goodies and buy the kids each one gift—all our budget would allow. Since we weren't going to Illinois for Christmas, all the grandparents had told us they were mailing packages with lots of toys for good girls and boys.

Monday morning dawned clear and cold, with just a few snowflakes drifting down to set the right mood for Christmas shopping. By time we had eaten our breakfast, however, the Endless Mountains in the distance had disappeared in a swirl of snow and the tombstones in the cemetery next door were buried. With a worried frown, Bill suggested, "I think we'd better wait and do our shopping tomorrow."

Every meteorologist knows that northern Pennsylvania's weather is capricious. Sweeping off the Great Lakes, where they gather huge amounts of moisture, the clouds then drop it all as they cross the mountains. Storms of 25 to 30 inches at a time were not at all uncommon. And it looked like we were in for a doozy.

The snow continued unabated all day. Amazed, we watched as our drive disappeared, then our road, and finally, our mailbox. Then our windows were gone, buried beneath piles of white stuff. We tried in vain to check outside, but 10-foot drifts blocked the front door. An eerie, dark silence settled over the parsonage as we burrowed down into our snow-blanketed cocoon.

We had pretty much emptied the larder already, baking and cooking for the church Christmas activities. Lavish eating or baking was not on the agenda until we got to the city grocery in Elmira. A few oranges left from our gift fruit basket, a little hamburger left from the Witties' gift, and some squeamy vegetables in the bottom of the freezer were all the kitchen would yield. Potatoes, carrots, and canned goods were in abundance in the garage, but we couldn't get the door open to fetch them.

We played games with the kids and listened to the radio—all those fun things everybody thinks they would enjoy doing while snowbound. But as the radio news began reporting snow depths of 56 inches, of homes burning down, and firefighters unable to get back the country roads to rescue them, our entrapment took on terrifying overtones.

No Christmas presents for the kids, no food for a holiday dinner, and not much wood in the house to keep the stove going. And the way things looked, there would be no more mail deliveries before Christmas, no chance for the grandparents' boxes to reach us.

Christmas Eve was dismal. We listened to carols on the radio— we were too far out in the country for television reception. Riggs was so small its zip code wasn't even a fraction; we, in fact, shared half a zip code each with Ulster and Milan. Ours was Milan, and the church, just down the hill, was on an Ulster route.

We tucked the kids in bed, piling them high with blankets and quilts against the cold, then climbed the stairs to our own cold bedroom. This was going to be a Christmas to remember but for all the wrong reasons. We knew the kids would bounce out of bed early, eager to open their gifts as they always did, so we tried to prepare them for the worst, telling them that Santa was using the postal service this year and probably couldn't get through the snow.

But we hadn't counted on the U.S. Postal Service. About noon on Christmas Day (a Saturday that year), we heard a mysterious scraping and blowing out by our front door. Puzzled, we waited, and the door finally crashed open, ushering in something that looked like the proverbial Abominable Snowman. Covered with frost and snow from head to foot, the apparition emerged and we recognized the face of Al Gordon, husband of the Milan postmistress in the valley below.

Tramping in behind him was his wife, Verna, laden with packages. "These came for you last night, and we knew you'd have a rotten Christmas up here on the mountain without them," she explained. "So we got out our tractor and plowed through."

Not only had the Gordons brought our Christmas packages, they had also loaded boxes full of groceries and baked goods, everything we needed to make a fantastic Christmas dinner.

At our insistence, they stayed and enjoyed dinner with us and watched the kids open their presents before heading back down the mountain, their errand of mercy complete. We thanked God for His wonderful provision, we thanked Him for wonderful friends like the Gordons, and we especially thanked Him that we shared our half of the Riggs zip code with Milan, where Verna was the postmistress.

Wit-n-Wisdom: Bethlehem was such a small town, they didn't even have a Pizza Hut—but they might have had a Little Caesar's.

CHAPTER 15

Blowin' in the Wind

*As you do not know the path of the wind ... so you cannot understand
the work of God, the Maker of all things. Ecclesiastes 11:5*

The storms continued to sweep across the Great Lakes. Howling winds and blowing snow persisted unabated for a couple of months. What originally had enchanted us like a winter wonderland became a relentless nightmare of trying to keep warm, keep the car out of the ditch, and keep everyone in the house healthy.

Our house sounded like a sanitarium, with all five of us coughing, whooping, and sneezing. It smelled even worse, with steam from vaporizers, Vicks, and rubbing alcohol permeating every crack and crevice.

Ray Dunn, a missionary to Liberia that our church helped support, came by for another service before his family returned to Africa. We gave him our electric blanket, then huddled our family together in one bed in a feeble attempt to stay warm under the other electric blanket. Ray came out of Billy's room the next morning, shaking with cold ... the bed where he had spent the night was covered with snow. "I've never been so cold in my entire life," he exclaimed.

We could completely sympathize. Snow had even piled into our living room, and we were all miserably cold. The thermometer was at about 10 below, and the wind was blowing at 60 mph, a combination that was nearly lethal to Bill. He went out into the storm to cut wood to try to heat the house and landed in the hospital. Dr. Fear, his cardiologist, said he couldn't figure out exactly what happened, but he narrowed it down to three possibilities: Bill suffered heart failure, which filled his lungs with fluid and caused pneumonia; his heart threw a blood clot into the lungs, causing heart failure; or heart failure created a strain on his blood vessels, causing hemorrhaging in the lungs. Whatever happened, it wasn't good and didn't portend well for Bill's future health.

He improved quickly, but the doctor insisted that Bill eat a very well-regulated diet, take a number of prescription medicines, and do absolutely no exercise, all virtually impossible in our particular living conditions.

That put me in charge of driving, something I've never been fond of. My philosophy of driving has always been, "It's like baseball. Nothing counts except the times you get home safely." Actually, I was afflicted with a dangerous disease called A.D.D.—acute driving disorder. I always preferred to drive from the passenger seat, letting Bill handle the nonessentials like shifting gears, clutching, and steering.

On my first run up to the hospital on the bad roads, Puny sputtered out right in the middle of an intersection on a blind curve. I tramped and tromped the accelerator until the car coughed and jumped into action. We went a bit farther, and Puny balked again, in the middle of the highest hill in East Smithfield. I choked him, tromped the accelerator, and hit every gadget on the dash. Still, he wouldn't budge. I tried backing down the hill, hoping the car would start once I got on the level. Still nothing. I finally got out and slammed the door, muttering, "I'll just leave the keys in the car and hope somebody's stupid enough to steal the dumb thing!"

I must have looked pretty funny hiking up that steep hill in the rain, snow, and fog, wearing high heels and toting a 20-pound baby!

A couple of weeks later after a church business meeting, we had to drive up to the Valley to get oil for the kitchen stove. Coming home, there wasn't a hill Puny could get up. We started up Laurel Hill and had to back down, then tried the lesser grade up the Milan blacktop. Even that was too much for him. Bill had to walk a long way through the storm to a telephone so he could call Nate Blow to come rescue us. The local garage owner towed Puny in the next day. He discovered a smashed gas line, where a rock had been thrown up and crushed it. Puny continued to act up, even leaving Bill stranded a few more times after that, another problem for his weak heart.

Because repairs to Puny were adding up so fast, we traded him for a 1965 Chevy Sportsvan, a nine-passenger bus that would be much handier for hauling all the kids. We got a good deal on the van, especially considering Studebaker had just gone defunct, leaving Puny an orphan with practically no resale value.

But the Sportsvan didn't handle the bad roads any better than his predecessor had. One night after church, we were hurrying into Kennedy's Market to buy Jeff some cereal before the store closed. Just around the curve from our house, a car ran us off the road, causing Bill to lose control in the mud. We tipped and swerved through the ditch for about forty or fifty yards, hitting an apple tree along the way, and nearly toppling over. Bill was thrown from the driver's seat and landed in my lap; Billy and Mari sailed across the back seat. Only Jeff in his car seat and I with my seat belt remained intact. Though none of us was seriously injured, we all ended up with a lot of bumps and bruises. We decided right then we would splurge on seat belts for both the rear seats.

The new van wasn't too badly damaged, except for some scratches, a bent mirror, and dented hubcaps. Stub brought the school bus to pull us out of the ditch, which was full of water. The man who had caused the accident stopped and gave us his name and insurance and promised to take care of our expenses. When we looked at the path the car had taken and the ditch full of water, we praised God for His protection. But Satan wasn't finished with his pranks just yet.

By time we got home (minus the cereal; the store was closed by then), our fire had gone out, and the house was freezing. Bill went out to split up some dry wood and I was in the bathroom, changing Jeff. Billy brought in an armload of wood, and the next thing I heard was Billy screaming hysterically. I rushed to the living room and found him rolling on the rug, flames shooting around him.

He had tried to light the fire with a little kerosene, and apparently there was still a spark left in the coals, because it blew up right in his face. His eyebrows and eyelashes were completely burned off, his hair was all singed, his ears and face were blistered badly, as were his lips and spots on his neck. Flames and sparks had burned holes in his shirt, but thankfully, it wasn't very flammable material. We praised God, too, that his Boy Scout training kicked in and he had the good sense to roll in the rug instead of running.

We tried to calm him down for more than an hour, trying to decide if we should take him up to the hospital, risking the dangerous snow-packed roads. He was hysterical and so odd acting we thought he may have gone into shock. We treated him with aspirin and first aid, then sat up and watched him the rest of the night, planning to make the hospital run in the morning when the roads hopefully would be safer.

Billy spent most of the next day in bed, just sitting and crying. I called the school nurse, who assured me all they would do at the hospital was what we had already done for him. She promised to check him at school the next day to make sure his eyeballs weren't burned. She said depression is common with a bad burn, and we should get him out with people right away to get his mind off it. But the poor little fellow looked so terrible he was ashamed for anyone to see him.

Even in such distress we could see God's hand. When Billy and Mari boarded the school bus the next day, he looked so frightful that the teens who had been bullying him all year took pity on him. Instead of the feared taunts and nastiness, the kids gave him candy, offered him a better seat, and became very protective of him. From that day on, they never teased him again, and he made a lot of new friends.

Because mountain travel involved as much pushing, shoveling, and digging out of ditches as actual driving, and because our church couldn't help us install an adequate oil furnace to keep Bill from having to chop wood, the RHMA leadership suggested we take a leave of absence from the field until Bill's heart was fixed.

Their second suggestion was for us to candidate at a small, struggling church near our home in East Peoria, where living wouldn't be so hard on Bill's heart. After much correspondence with Rev. Longenecker over the next couple of months, we made the tough decision to leave the field. Bill would candidate at the Germantown church while we were back for conference, and I would go to work in the home office.

But on March 8, Bill wrote a letter to the director:

> *Adell and I have some news that you may receive with mixed emotions. Since we had made the decision to leave the field here, neither of us has had any peace of mind, but did not convey our feelings to each other. This last Tuesday, Adell was at a banquet in Towanda and I was child caring when the urgent need of praying the matter through came upon me.*

> *After a few minutes of prayer, I said yes to God—I was willing to stay. God removed the burden and when Adell came home I told her the news, and she readily agreed.*

> *Friday, I talked with the new heart specialist at Packer and he assured me that surgery would be necessary in a year or two, but advised that I go ahead as I am, if that is what we want. He did not feel it would cause any difficulty.*

> *The church voted to keep us 15 to 2, so maybe the family that's been causing the trouble will cease.*

Just a few days later we received Rev. Longenecker's gracious reply, stating: *It was surprising, but not shocking news. I am glad the decision was made by you, altogether on your own and without any persuasion from us. We want you to have perfect liberty to do as the Lord directs.*

The church was growing every week; at our annual Watch Night Service on New Year's Eve, several had rededicated their lives to Christ and a couple got saved. Chet Decker came forward and said, "I'm claiming Phil. 4:13 as my verse for the New Year. With God's help, I've smoked my last cigarette." One of the families who had caused so much trouble repented and "bent over backwards" to make up for all the dissension they had brought. With the Lord working among our people, we just couldn't accept that God wanted us to leave so soon.

God confirmed our decision a few days after Bill wrote to the mission. The Electro-Mechanical Corp. in Sayre called and offered Bill an executive position as a planner. After much prayer and with the approval of our deacons and the RHMA, we felt this was God's answer to our problem. Dr. Fear, of course, was delighted with what he termed "an ideal situation." Bill would be sitting behind a desk all day, eating properly, and not having to do all the wood chopping chores since we could afford to put in oil heat.

Actually, the situation was too ideal as far as we were concerned. Having become accustomed to living on virtually no income and having to trust God literally for our daily bread, we worried about making too much money. Rev. Longenecker counseled us to use the money Bill earned to pay off past medical bills and put the rest in the bank toward the future surgery. Wisely, he told us not to drop any of our supporters, because if we had to move to another field, it would be very difficult to pick up support again.

Further, he cautioned, "if people stop supporting you, they'll also stop praying for your ministry, and right now you need all the prayer you can get!"

We felt a little uneasy accepting donations from so many folks who gave sacrificially to keep us on the field, but we could see the wisdom of our director's advice. I was so torn about it, I wrote to Mom, my "sounding board": *I almost wish Bill were working for about $40 a week, which would buy his medicine and proper diet things like his salt and sugar substitutes, fresh produce, and lots of lean meat—no more cheap casseroles! That would still keep us dependent upon our supporters, but keep the wolves at bay, too. Anyway, we're in a frustrated state of indecision, so please pray for us.*

Several months earlier, the PTA had asked Bill to be area chairman for the Cub Scouts, and I became a Den Mother. The Sunday School Association elected him chairman for its annual convention, and the pastors' fellowship appointed him secretary of their group. Which meant, in addition to pastoring a busy church, he had a lot on his plate already—and now he was taking a full-time, 40-hour a week job. While it did help immensely in the financial department, the job brought more stresses. Driving to the office every morning in the subzero cold, with gale-force winds and high snowdrifts, was still more work than pleasure.

Often, he'd have to go out to the doorless garage, pull out the battery, and then haul it in by the stove to warm it up so the car would start. And, of course, driving still included as much snow shoveling and ditch maneuvering as it had. "But," he admonished me, "at least now I'm getting paid for it!"

As January, February, and March rolled on, we began to think of it not as "The Land of the Endless Mountains" but as "The Land of the Endless Snow." We were once again snowbound, with all the roads leading to our house blocked by huge drifts. The kerosene supply for the kitchen stove ran out, leaving temperatures in that part of the house near the freezing point.

The snow blew in to our doorless garage with a fury, totally covering our wood supply. We soon learned that soggy wet wood didn't burn very well and fervently wished our church members had agreed to put doors on the garage when we had asked them to. We were all coughing and shaking with cold, but the worst was yet to come.

Bill exhausted his supply of fluid pills and was literally drowning in his own fluids. He could barely breathe, gasping for every hard-earned breath; his legs swelled and the skin burst from the excessive fluid accumulating in his body. But we were snowbound once again, unable to get to the drugstore to refill his prescription. We were beginning to get desperate, praying hard that God would send relief. Finally, our nearest neighbor, who also happened to be the township road commissioner, managed to plow a road grader across a wind-swept field, bypassing the drifted road.

We all looked on in awe as Johnny plowed the big grader almost to our door. Bill grabbed a corner of the huge machine, swinging himself into the cab like Tarzan. He held on for dear life as Johnny plowed back the way he had come. They took the grader all the way into a main road in East Smithfield, where a truck was waiting to take Bill to the hospital.

We weren't able to have church for two weeks during that particular storm. On the third Sunday, a freezing rain "polished up" the roads, keeping attendance down again. Never had I seen so much snow at one time, even when we had lived in Milwaukee, where the snow piled up on the streets so bad we ran our car antenna up and tied a flag to it so we could be seen at intersections.

Here, an ordinary car antenna couldn't have been seen over the 10- to 12-foot heaps. When they finally managed to get our roads opened part way, the snow banks were so high it felt like we were driving through a tunnel. Of course, as soon as the wind began blowing, the snow blew off the huge piles and blocked our roads again.

The kids had to walk through the snow tunnels to catch the school bus down at the main road, and I daily worried that they'd get lost in an avalanche if the cornices collapsed.

Easter was on April 10 that year, relatively late in the season, yet it was still snowing. Despite the snow, which had come down for eighteen days straight during that particular storm, nearly 1,200 people crowded into the area memorial park for the 17th annual Easter sunrise service. Bill had been asked to direct the entire program and to be the main speaker. It was the largest crowd he had ever preached to, and he was understandably nervous.

Despite spending a sleepless night tossing and turning, he did a magnificent job of presenting the glorious news of the resurrection and seemed very composed and professional. It was a remarkable service, complete with Carillotine chimes, trumpet solos, and Posting of the Colors by the Towanda American Legion. A highlight was the flight of the doves, an inspiring release of a flock of doves from the bell tower.

The Memorial Association manager called us later that morning to tell us he'd received many favorable reports, and that "folks said it was the best service they'd had yet."

We had fifty-two in Sunday School Easter morning, thirty more than the previous Easter. The church was so small, fifty-two people really looked like a huge crowd. Another family came forward to join the church, and a teenage girl asked Jesus into her heart. That night, fifty-four came out for the evening service.

It was still snowing as we prepared to head back to Illinois for the annual RHMA conference the week after Easter. Apparently, we were all getting accustomed to the winter driving: Church attendance continued to climb, youth group had record attendances, and prayer meeting and Sunday evening services were well attended.

We couldn't wait to share with our flatland friends and supporters all that God had done. We worked hard on a missionary display showing our ministry in the Endless Mountains. The Chamber of Commerce gave us lots of "freebies" to advertise the beautiful area; local sugar farmers gave us maple sugar candy shaped like leaves to distribute; the Area Craft Association gave us native woodcarvings and basket weavings from pine needles for our display.

Best of all was the statistic sheet we prepared—thirty-three souls were born into the Kingdom, eight young people dedicated their lives to Christ; attendance increased 155 percent; church membership was up by 50 percent; six people had been baptized, with another group waiting to be baptized. And to cap it all, the church had to purchase the house next door as a Sunday School annex to handle the fast-growing Sunday School! All in all, it had been a very good year and a half.

But Satan wasn't about to take all this progress sitting down. Two days before we planned to leave for Illinois, Bill could barely get out of bed. Something had slipped out of place in his lower back, putting him in terrible agony. Nevertheless, he attempted to go to work, where they sent him right to the doctor. Dosed up with painkillers and muscle relaxers, he made it home, but every move just about tore him apart.

Mari woke up with a bad earache the same morning, and Jeff cried half the night with a sore throat. How could we possibly drive back to Illinois? We had made such elaborate preparations, had several services lined up, and felt like we really had to go. We prayed fervently that God would work it out.

Bill's pain subsided somewhat, so we decided to make the trip. By time we got to Illinois, Bill was rather a sorry sight, hobbling around, looking somewhat like the Hunchback of Notre Dame. On Thursday night, he was scheduled to tell about our work in the Endless Mountains at conference. As he mounted the platform, he joked, "I've only been with the RHMA three years, and just look at what it's done to me!"

By the next day, the pain was so intense he didn't feel much like joking, and the doctor ordered him to bed. By Saturday, the doctor decided to admit him to the hospital to prepare for our long trip home. When I called a couple of the pastors who had invited us to speak at their churches to tell them we wouldn't be able to come, they answered, "Well, we're prepared for a missionary speaker, so why don't you come and share with us?" That was my first introduction to public speaking, knocking knees and all.

I learned to do a lot of things that month. With Bill lying in misery in a makeshift bed in the backseat, I drove all the way home through a spring snowstorm. We had a couple of close calls but no major calamities. I thought my bad driving would scare away Bill's pain, but no such luck! As soon as we got home, I had to take him to the hospital, where they harnessed him up in traction with plans to keep him there for several weeks.

In addition to public speaking and winter driving, I also had to learn to keep a fire burning in the cantankerous stove and haul in wood, though I never did master the art of chopping it.

Bill, who majored in accounting and business at college, had always done our finances, taking care of tax forms, balancing the checkbook, all that nuisance stuff. About all I knew about our financial situation was that it was fluid—going down the drain. With him laid up in the hospital for so long, I had to pay the bills and balance the checkbook. One day I proudly showed him the checkbook so he could see what a good job I was doing. He looked it over and then gave me a puzzled look. "What are all these ESP notations?"

"Oh, that's where I had to use my powers of ESP to make it balance."

He jerked up in bed, rattling the chains that were holding his "body cradle" in the traction contraption. "You used ESP to balance the checkbook?" he thundered.

Meekly I replied, "ESP is shorthand for 'Error Some Place.'"

We looked at Bill's enforced downtime as a blessing rather than a burden. The doctors said he desperately needed to slow down for his heart's sake. What better place to pull the props out and land him in a predicament where he had no choice but to rest? The nurses could do a much better job of hog-tying him than I could!

As usual when I needed her, Mom came out to stay with us and help carry the load. My public speaking experiences while we were at conference convinced me I shouldn't inflict my speaking on our church folks, so I made arrangements with a Bible School in New York to send pulpit supply each week—a big mistake as far as our checkbook was concerned. The first week, our treasurer gave me our weekly check of $11.44. I turned around and wrote out a check for $15 to the Bible School student who filled the pulpit that Sunday. At that rate, I wouldn't have to worry about balancing the checkbook—I could just write in"0" and close the account.

Wit-n-Wisdom: What the storms of life do to us depends upon what life finds in us. Paul and Jonah both went through a storm, but their circumstances were quite different.

CHAPTER 16

Ordination, Weddings, and Kids

You have not chosen me, but I have chosen you, and ordained you, that you should go and bring forth fruit, and that your fruit should remain. John 15:16

During Rev. Longenecker's field visit with us the previous fall, he had suggested that Bill start considering ordination. Our first thought was that he should be ordained from our home church, the one that had commissioned us for missionary service.

Our home pastor, however, discouraged us. "You've only been a pastor for a couple of years. You really need to prepare more, get more experience under your belt," he said. "I'm not sure you're ready for such a big step."

Disheartened, we sent the pastor's letter to Rev. Longenecker for his opinion. Trying to be gracious in his reply, Rev. Longenecker wrote something to the effect of, "Is he nuts?!" He went on to encourage us, saying Bill's required doctrinal statement when we applied to the RHMA was one of the most concise and well-documented he had ever received. Biblically, he said, the church where Bill was serving as pastor should be the one to ordain him anyway.

Our folks jumped on that bandwagon immediately. Over the years, they had ordained a number of young people to ministry and were excited by the opportunity to do it again. They pointed out it

137

was good timing. Lauralee, one of our young girls, was planning to get married that summer when she and her fiancé graduated from Bible college. "You need to be ordained right away, Pastor," they said, "so you can legally perform the wedding."

As was customary in our Baptist churches, the church clerk sent an invitation to fellow pastors throughout the twin tiers of southern New York and northern Pennsylvania, calling for an ordination council. The ladies began baking goodies for the event, and we all pitched in to get the church and newly annexed fellowship hall "spit and polished" for the grand occasion.

There was a catch. Bill was still hospitalized, hanging in traction. We prayed and prayed he would be released in time for the soon-coming council on May 26. He spent his time in the hospital studying, trying to read his Bible and commentaries while suspended a few feet above the bed in something they called a "cradle traction." Taking notes was impossible from that position, so he tried hard to memorize everything. Sometimes I sat by his bedside, pen and notebook in hand, taking down in shorthand things he needed to remember.

The doctors put him in a full body cast May 20, and he got to come downstairs at the hospital to see the kids. What a happy reunion! Baby Jeff had almost forgotten who he was and shied away from him at first.

The next day I got a call from Bill, his voice shaking with excitement. "They said I can come home! Hurry and get up here before they change their minds!" he said.

Things were once again looking up. We had already scheduled a pulpit supply for Bill, but he decided to attend Sunday services anyway, despite the body cast. He had difficulty sitting, so he stood for most of the service. At home, he had to sleep in the recliner Mom had bought him earlier. We actually cleared $1.51 after paying the pulpit supply that week.

Rev. Rice, our spiritual mentor and teacher, arrived on Tuesday from Wisconsin to begin a week of special meetings centered around Bill's ordination. He and Bill drove to Sayre to tape daily radio broadcasts, then spent the rest of the day reminiscing and talking about the Lord's goodness.

Thursday afternoon, cars began pulling into the church parking lot before noon. Grace Baptist Annex was a beehive of activity as our ladies prepared to feed the huge crowd of pastors and messengers from the numerous churches.

The pastors took their responsibility seriously, questioning Bill on just about everything they thought he might encounter. They wanted his views on every conceivable doctrine, practical ministerial matters, and his personal life. One of the pastors, enjoying the moment, asked, "How many angels can dance on the head of a pin?"

Afterward, several remarked: "This is the most congenial, friendly ordination council I've ever attended, and I've taken part in many of them!"

There was a lot of laughter and levity, especially when a pastor who didn't know Bill's health situation asked, "If your health failed or you had financial problems, would you be able to stick it out?"

The crowd roared with laughter as Bill hobbled to his feet and pointed to the body cast beneath his suit. "I'm still here, aren't I?"

The council moderator explained some of the circumstances Bill had gone through, and added, "I've never met anyone with as much fortitude, faith, and perseverance in the light of hardships as this man has already demonstrated. If anyone is worthy of ordination, Bill Farley surely is."

Bill wasn't too comfortable sitting for more than three hours with the itchy cast on, but I was so proud of him. Even I was surprised at the depth of his spiritual understanding and knowledge, and I had been enjoying his preaching and teaching for three years. He said he got grilled for three hours and came out toasted. The council voted unanimously to recommend that the church ordain him, so on their authority, the service was planned for Sunday afternoon.

May 29, 1966, was no doubt the crowning day of Bill's life. Grant Rice preached the ordination service, which was especially appropriate since he was instrumental in Bill's decision to become a minister. Some of our RHMA missionaries joined us for the occasion, including our field director from Jersey Mills and the radio director from Lancaster, Bill and Emma Horst. Along with my Mom and the Rices, it made for a very crowded parsonage that week. But the fellowship was so sweet, we didn't do a whole lot of sleeping anyway.

The next edition of the *RHMA Messenger* carried a story about Bill's ordination, including testimonials from some of the people from the church:

> *"Thirty some years ago, when we built this church, we took as our verse, 'If this work be of men, it will come to naught; but if it be of God, ye cannot overthrow it.' For a while, it looked as though it WOULD come to nothing…. We didn't know where to turn. But then the RHMA sent Mr. Farley out, and things really picked up"* (from a deacon).

> *"This church has sent out over twenty men into full-time Christian service and has had several ordinations like this one. Maybe that's why Satan tried so hard to defeat the work here. It almost died, until Brother Farley arrived two years ago. Our hearts are thrilled to learn of the growth that has taken place since then"* (from a former pastor).

Many similar comments were made at the service, comments that just about "blessed our socks off." We were thrilled and humbled by the letters that came from afar, by the testimonials of our own church folk, and the remarks by our fellow pastors. But we knew we didn't deserve such accolades—they belonged to the faithful people who had stood with us in prayer and held the ropes for us.

Those prayers were still very much needed as we coped with Bill's health issues. His back didn't improve as quickly as the doctors thought it should, and they told him it might take six months for full recovery—which meant a long time for me to try to keep him down. He still walked sort of humped over and couldn't climb the stairs to our bedroom, so he spent his nights in the recliner. On June 3, I drove Mom to the train station in Waverly, sad to see her leave. With Bill still laid up, I really needed her helping hands.

VBS time came, long before I was ready for it. Mom wanted to stay and help with our VBS, but she was needed to help with her own church summer VBS and camping programs in Illinois. Bill was scheduled to go back to work full-time, and I wondered how I was going to handle everything. When he went back to Dr. Mirtland for his checkup before returning to work, they talked about their respective VBS programs. "Isn't your VBS coming up next week?" the doctor asked.

To Bill's affirmative reply, Dr. Mirtland grinned and said, "I really think you need another week or two off work. Let's keep you home until VBS is over." God worked it out far better than we could have imagined. Not only was Bill available to help with VBS, the school district paid us $5 a day to haul kids to a special reading and remedial program, four days a week, funded by President Johnson's anti-poverty program.

We thought the anti-poverty initiative at the school would keep many of our kids away from VBS, but we averaged more than seventy every day for the two weeks. Seven more children made decisions for Christ, and we saw some minor miracles among our old timers. One of our men, who previously had refused even to stop and pick up children on his way to church, came to me and asked if he could have a route to pick up kids for VBS. For two weeks, he traipsed all over the countryside, gathering kids for VBS.

And our very shy lady, who rarely spoke up, did a tremendous job teaching the teenagers. She got them studying and working and so excited about the class that they all came back daily without a single dropout for the entire two weeks. I taught the kindergarten class, figuring I could keep 1-year-old Jeff out of trouble there.

Meanwhile, I had a houseful of kids once school ended for the summer. We became legal guardians for Margie, a 12-year-old girl whose mother had gone to jail, and had another little girl stay with us every day while her mother worked. Church families continued to bring me their kids to watch, since I was "going to be home anyway." The parsonage was literally bursting at the seams with activity, and I thought I would go berserk.

Nearly every day I had ten or twelve kids underfoot, sometimes until late in the evening. With Bill back at work, I drove his route for the summer school, hampered by road construction. The main road to Milan was torn up, a dusty, dirty mess, and often I had to sit and wait for the construction workers to clear a traffic lane. To expedite traffic, they finally got smart and set up a detour around Laurel Hill.

The detour proved to be a marvelous blessing to my child-weary soul. Laurel Hill, a gorgeous lane meandering through deep woods and down a steep hill, was abloom with mountain laurel and rhododendron, a spectacular garden beyond description. I eagerly looked forward to my daily quiet time in what I considered "God's garden," while Margie was an excellent babysitter with Jeff every morning.

Those quiet moments prepared me for the hectic day ahead and were a real balm to my spirit. Margie proved to be a great help in many ways. Coming from a tragic dysfunctional home, she had mothered her two younger brothers for years and given them the only security they knew. She mended, she cooked, she cleaned. We tried to shower her with love, explaining that she didn't have to work so hard—she was now our daughter, no matter what. She was a great influence on Mari, who enjoyed working alongside her "big sister," washing dishes and learning to bake.

Margie had only been with us a few weeks when her dad came by and asked if we could also take Johnny, Margie's 11-year-old brother. He offered to pay for Johnny's board and expenses at $7 a week. The poor father was in a terrible predicament, with his ex-wife threatening to burn down his house and the Welfare Department threatening to take the children away from him if he didn't provide a more stable home for them. His mother offered to care for his youngest son, but she was in no position to take the older two.

When the kids' mother ended up in jail, Bill wanted to adopt all three kids and began praying about the possibility. Jerry, the youngest, stayed with us frequently, as did a cousin who also had a bad family situation.

While directing VBS, caring for kids, and transporting the summer school kids, we also had a wedding to plan. The wedding was scheduled for the Saturday right in the middle of VBS. We were hosting the out-of-town guests for the bridal couple and also giving the rehearsal dinner at the parsonage. The timing couldn't have been worse; we had to take down all our VBS decorations and classrooms for the wedding, then put them all back up again for the following week.

I also was to play for the wedding, music that was way out of my expertise level, so every spare minute I could find I spent practicing. That same week, one of our new ladies had to have breast surgery at the Geisinger Clinic down in Danville, 80 miles away, and needed Bill to pray with her. I tried to get him to stay home and just let me drive down myself, but he wouldn't hear of it. Once he got an idea in his head, there was no stopping him; he refused to believe he was an invalid.

The night before the wedding, the entire wedding party—minus the bride, of course—stayed with us, plus the relatives of the groom. We were up until after 1 a.m., with everyone taking turns in the single bathroom trying to get ready for bed. On Saturday morning, it really got hectic. Primping bridesmaids tied up the bathroom all morning, and Bill and I were flying around hauling chairs from the school, setting up the church, and decorating, in addition to preparing breakfast for all our guests.

In the midst of all the hustle and bustle, we listened to the bridesmaids griping and complaining about the "backwoods wedding," wondering why Lauralea hadn't planned to get married in their big city church. Despite all the problems, the wedding was beautiful, and Lauralea was a composed, gorgeous bride. That's more than you could say for me, the harried, hassled preacher's wife!

We helped with the reception, which was provided by the ladies from our church, and just assumed that some of the bride's and groom's relatives had put things back in order at the church. Wrong assumption. We arrived for Sunday School the next morning to a big mess. We had to haul the chairs back to the school, rearrange the sanctuary, and even rehang the curtains. Someone had just piled them on the floor in one of the Sunday School rooms along with the floral boxes and other trash.

The bride's father later handed Bill $5 "for being so nice." At that moment, we didn't feel "so nice" and often joked with each other about our $5 Endless Mountain Wedding Plan. Once again God reminded us not "to be weary in well doing, for in due season you will reap if you faint not." Our reward was far more valuable than money. One of the groomsmen, a recent Bible college graduate, was interested in rural work, so we loaded him down with brochures and information about the RHMA. The bridal couple later became missionaries with the RHMA themselves, serving a rural church in Kansas.

An old adage says, "There's no rest for the weary, and the righteous don't need any." We didn't know which category described us, but we were certainly getting weary. The VBS picnic was planned for Friday following the wedding, another girl was getting married at the church Friday night, Saturday was the couples club picnic, Sunday was our VBS closing program and open house, and two families from our main supporting church were coming for a vacation with us on Monday. The week after that, Bill's folks were coming to visit from Illinois.

A family who had read our story in *Christian Life* magazine came for a visit from southern Pennsylvania, bringing Christmas in July. The RHMA's office manager, Gil Busenitz, also stopped by on his way from helping to move RHMA missionaries from Alabama to Michigan. With so many guests, we didn't have time to worry about being tired; we just enjoyed all the fellowship and a lot of great sightseeing as we gave many of them the grand tour of our gorgeous mountains.

Everyone who came brought gifts for the kids, accepting Margie and Johnny as just two more of our kids. We had already begun to think of them as ours, and Bill told his folks, "It's hard to believe how you can get so attached to somebody else's kids so fast. They're just like our own." They fit right in with our family, although Johnny was awfully insecure and frustrated. The more they told us about their life, the more unbelievable it was that the authorities hadn't removed the kids from the home. Their mother had gone to jail once for attacking Margie with a butcher knife. The neighbors heard her screaming and called the police, who carried the mother away in handcuffs. The mother tried to burn down the house a couple of times, and things went from bad to worse.

Shortly after Margie and Johnny came to live with us, their mother was sentenced to two years at the New York State Penitentiary for manslaughter, stemming from a drunken driving accident. That news was actually a relief to us, knowing that we wouldn't have to contend with her for a while. Thanks to a praying grandmother, the kids were remarkably unscathed and well adjusted.

Margie and Johnny's situation made us acutely aware of the home problems so many kids endured. It brought us face to face with the Welfare Department, which shared their tale of woe with us. There were so many kids that had to be taken away from parents that the state couldn't find foster homes fast enough. And the foster homes it did find often were as bad or worse than the homes the children had been taken from. It had gotten so bad that the state was using a couple of rooms at the county nursing home for temporary housing for the backlog of kids.

My ever-lovin', softhearted husband had the solution. Our big old barn of a house was so big, and we had so much love to share, why didn't we just open a children's home? The Welfare Department thought it sounded like a great solution to its problem and started checking into the idea.

I was ready to go along with anything Bill thought was in God's plan for us, but my insecurities came out in a letter to Mom: *Can't you see me, with my tremendous lack of patience, trying to raise a houseful of problem kids? It's surprising, though, but since Margie's been here, I don't holler nearly so much. She's a good settling influence. Mostly, because I know she's never known anything but yelling and screaming, I'm trying to teach her that ladies don't yell. Which brings it home to roost every time I open my mouth to bellow at somebody or something.*

Bill and the local welfare authorities continued to explore the possibilities of our opening a home for children, only to be hit by proverbial brick walls everywhere we turned. We visited a couple of Christian children's homes in southern Pennsylvania—lovely, spacious homes with all the conveniences and amenities one could want, yet the state was trying to shut them down. One of the directors told us that both the state and federal governments were butting in, attempting to close down all religious homes.

"Kids are sleeping on the floor in the County Children's Home because of lack of beds, yet our beautiful home isn't good enough!" Ed raged. In some areas, the Welfare Department was housing kids in the county jail, he said. Meanwhile, a number of religious homes had been shut down in southern Pennsylvania because they couldn't keep up with the stringent regulations the state was imposing on them.

Bill later met with a state representative of the Welfare Department, who told him precisely what we had already learned in Lancaster County. The state was forcing private homes out of business with its restrictive rules in an attempt to close down all religious children's homes. "I personally feel it's a very bad move," he told Bill. "But I'm not in a position to fight it. All we can do up here is try to do the best we can for the kids."

There was a desperate need for a specialized foster home for teenagers in our county, he said, urging Bill to make an application. That way we could take up to ten kids and not have to fight the state regulations, plus the Welfare Department would pay for their keep. Bill sensed the department was eager and anxious to work with us, as it would help alleviate its problem of finding housing for the teens. Was this the direction God wanted us to go? It would be a stopgap place for the teens, and we realized there would be a constant turnover as the foster teens came and went. What an opportunity to reach many for the Lord! We immediately got down on our prayer bones and asked for God's leadership.

Wit-n-Wisdom: Faith either removes mountains or tunnels through them.

CHAPTER 17

Cantankerous Saints and Other Blessings

*Look not every man on his own things, but every man
also on the things of others. Philippians 2:4*

very church has its share of cranky saints, and Grace
Baptist was no exception. Our treasurer could be one of
the sweetest, most loving ladies around, but when she got
an idea in her head, she hung onto it with the tenacity of a bulldog.
For some reason, she was adamant that the church couldn't afford
to install a furnace or even a space heater in the parsonage. "The
preacher can get his own wood like the rest of us have to do!" she
often declared.

When the temperature dipped down to 36 degrees in July and
frost covered the garage roof, we knew Bill was in for another terrible
year of wood chopping and hauling. We had both wood stoves going
full blast, and we were still shivering in the big old barn-like house.
Bill's heart had much improved due to his enforced rest in the body
cast, but the heart specialist had warned him that he couldn't survive
another winter of hard physical labor.

Most of our church folks were concerned, especially when they
experienced the chill for themselves when they visited us at the

parsonage. "We've got to do something about getting a furnace in here," they often said.

My mom's church, Oak Grove Evangelical Bible Church, offered to pay our monthly heating bills if our church would install an oil furnace. But nobody was willing to take on the treasurer at our monthly business meetings. She had firmly declared the previous year there was no way the church could afford to buy a furnace, and that was that.

One of the men cautiously brought up the subject at the trustees' meeting one Sunday. Betty declared, "We don't have the money, so there's no use discussing anything about a furnace! Like I've said before, the pastor can get his own wood like the rest of us." Causing more stir than a nest of disturbed hornets, she finally stomped out of the meeting.

To restore the peace, Bill offered to put in our own space heater. We went to Sears to see if we could find an oil space heater that would work and found one for $454, an enormous sum for our limited budget. Bill talked to the local banker about getting a personal loan to cover it, knowing that if he quit his job we'd be strapped to pay a monthly payment. What to do? We even considered moving out of the cold, drafty parsonage and buying ourselves a mobile home that would be warmer. Then someone suggested that the church sell the parsonage and use the money from it to buy a trailer that would be fuel-efficient. Feelings were running high and Satan was having a field day.

The heat situation was to be the main topic of discussion at the regular monthly business meeting, a meeting we dreaded. The conflict and rancor were palpable, and what had once been congenial, fun business meetings had deteriorated to arguing and bickering sessions.

Bill was late getting home from work, and we were rushing around trying to get supper over with before the business meeting. Just as we sat down to eat, the phone rang. It was our church treasurer, asking Bill to come over to the hospital right away. Her husband had broken his back in a fall from the haymow. While Bill drove to the Troy Hospital, I called around and cancelled the business meeting, asking everyone to pray for Winfield.

Bill stayed with the family and didn't get home that night until after 11, then went back again the following day after work. The Troy Hospital was miles away in the opposite direction of his numerous hospital visits in Sayre; we also had patients down in Towanda and some in Elmira. Bill firmly believed a pastor should visit his people and tried to get all his visits in after working all day. That schedule didn't leave much time for studying and sermon preparation, and he seriously considered quitting his full-time desk job. But then we couldn't pay for a space heater, without which he would spend all his time chopping wood. It seemed to be a vicious cycle, which kept our thought pattern "going around in circles."

With Winfield laid up with a broken back, "the preacher who could get his own wood like the rest of us had to" found himself not only getting his own wood, but doing chores for the injured man. Bill called for a workday to get Winfield's hay in, but only Bill and his dad, who was visiting us on his vacation, plus one other young man from church showed up. Our ladies provided food for the workers, but the men were busy getting their own hay in.

"I'll bet these guys would sure appreciate it if someone helped them when they were in a position like Winfield, and the shoe was on the other foot," Dad Farley grumbled. His grumbling was almost prophetic. I went to pick up food at Stub's house, only to find them gone. To the hospital. One of their heifers had horned Stub that morning and mauled him over, injuring his arm and bruising him badly.

I couldn't help my nasty thoughts. "If he had come over to help Winfield, he might not have had a hospital bill." As it was, he spent the entire day at the hospital, and the preacher spent the next Saturday getting Stub's haying done.

Satan continued to buffet our people with accidents and illnesses. A teenager was dying with leukemia; a young mother of six children discovered a large lump in her breast, just after her husband ran off with another woman. Most nights Bill stopped on his way home from work to make several hospital calls at Packer and then drove over to Troy to see Winfield or to help with their chores.

The teen with leukemia was in the Troy hospital as well. His strength was failing fast, and the doctors doubted he would live more than a few more days. Bill talked to him a little while, but the boy could barely talk. When Bill explained the plan of salvation and asked him if he would like to receive Jesus, Don brightened up and exclaimed, "Yes, I would! Right now!" Bill led him in the sinner's prayer, just as his mother flounced in and declared, "I know a little bit about the Bible, and it says God loves everyone. He loves all good boys, and my Donnie is a good boy. He doesn't need your sinner's talk."

Bill was totally dejected when he got home that night. The woman was so angry with him, she refused to let him come back to visit again. Later, we heard some of the rumors she spread around the area, telling people that "Mr. Farley kicked the family out of Donnie's room so he could preach at him," and all sorts of other nonsense.

On the home front, things weren't exactly easy either. My friend Marge was helping the young mother who had breast cancer, and whenever she spent the day with her at the hospital, I watched her kids along with my own growing brood. That usually meant I was caring for at least ten or eleven kids every day. "Good preparation for running the children's home," Bill teased.

In the midst of all this, the doctors told us Billy had to have his right thumb operated on or he would totally lose control of that hand. When Billy was born, the doctor did the routine exam, making sure everything was normal. The evening we took him home from the hospital, Bill was holding him. Suddenly he exclaimed, "Dollie! Come quick. He's got two thumbs!"

"No kidding," I replied. "Everybody's got two thumbs!"

"No, I mean Billy's got two thumbs on one hand!"

I rushed over to see what my crazy husband was talking about. Sure enough, my "perfect" little son had two thumbs growing out of his right hand. How we all had missed it earlier, I'll never know. But the doctor advised us to have what seemed to be the excess thumb removed. We thought they would use X-rays and check it out, but when we took him back to the hospital, the doctor just chopped one of the thumbs off, stitched it, and covered it with a small bandage.

As Billy grew, we noticed his remaining thumb was pulling awkwardly away from his hand, and several more minor surgeries followed. Now, however, the orthopedic surgeons felt it was time to do a major overhaul, including resetting the top joint on top of the bottom one and using plastic surgery to loosen the tight skin that was pulling his thumb so far out of whack. They warned us it would be a "very long, tedious operation." Billy was scheduled for surgery at the Guthrie Clinic on Aug. 17 to give him time to recover before school started.

And I needed time to recover before his surgery! My kidneys began acting up, and I suffered some of the worst pain I'd ever felt. Dr. Corner said my cold had settled in my kidneys, producing a bad infection. He ordered me to bed rest, something that was nearly impossible. On Sunday, we had the Snyder family from Bolivia; on Tuesday, our field director brought a couple that were mutual friends of ours for supper. They all decided to spend the night, so I had 15 people to find beds and pajamas for.

That crew didn't leave until about one the next afternoon, and at two o'clock two couples from the Pittsburgh area arrived. Normally I would have enjoyed hosting so many folks, but I was so sick and in such pain I could barely think straight.

Each group of visitors brought us "Christmas in August," inundating all of us with box after box of gifts. Tablecloths, pillowcases, towels, a lamp, badminton set, greeting cards, hand cream, cosmetics, aftershave, groceries—we were overwhelmed with their generosity. They even brought fudge and cookies for the kids and special notepaper for me. Every time I started grousing and grumping, God sent along special blessings to calm me down.

Billy and Johnny went to one of our farmer's for a campout, enjoying a boys' weekend before he had to go in for the surgery. They set up tents way back in the woods and hauled off a ton of snacks and goodies to fortify them through the long, scary weekend—their very first time alone in the woods.

Having the boys gone a couple of days may have helped; at any rate, the kidney infection cleared up in time for me to spend the day at the hospital for Billy's surgery.

We had just managed to pay our van off and were counting on Bill's work checks to clear up the enormous bills from his back problems. As soon as that was paid, he planned to quit work. And now we were facing more big bills for Billy's hand surgery. As the saying goes, "We were getting behinder and behinder." It seemed we would never reach the point where Bill would feel financially able to quit work.

We went ahead with plans to buy our own space heater and had Sears come out with an estimate. But the estimator told us a space heater wouldn't be practical for the parsonage, leaving us with yet another quandary. A space heater we could sell when God called us elsewhere, but should we invest a lot of money in a furnace that would have to stay in the house? At that time, I was just angry enough at those who insisted Bill get his own wood and stubborn enough not to want to donate a furnace to them!

How God, and Bill, put up with all my complaining is a mystery to me. Through it all, Bill maintained a peaceful and loving attitude. He wrote to Rev. Longenecker, "I've relegated my heart condition to the back of my mind, and urge you to do the same. We're not going to let it keep us from going wherever or doing whatever the Lord leads, and will cross the surgery bridge when and if we come to it."

"Relegating" his heart condition to the back of his mind, Bill continued to get wood in for Winfield, help Stub with his chores, build closets in the parsonage for our extra children, and work full time. I nagged and nagged, but had to give it up because of my throat. He threatened to slit it! No amount of nagging or cajoling could keep my determined husband down, and I worried as his breathing got so bad we had to stack the head of our bed up on blocks to help him breathe.

We continued to meet with the Welfare Department and state officials about setting up a foster home for teens. Meanwhile, we made certain that the children God had already put in our home were having a good time. We even took them bear hunting. A huge six-foot black bear took up residence at the Ridgebury dump, and everyone said he was quite friendly and put on a show every night for the crowds who went to see him. To make sure our kids didn't miss out on the fun, we drove over to the dump late one night and spent a scary night at the dark, deserted dump, waiting for Bruno to show up. Not wanting to waste the trip, Bill had loaded our trash in the back of the car. As he got out of the car to unload it, the kids were all whispering, "Be careful, Daddy! There's a big bear out there!"

"Do not hand feed the bear" and "Keep children away from the bear" signs were all over the place, and we were disappointed that Bruno didn't show up. But we enjoyed a fun, if scary, night together.

On Labor Day weekend, we took a six-hour trip to the Jersey Shore so Johnny, Margie, and Jerry could see the ocean for the first time. Jerry, especially, was impressed. "Wow! That ocean is a whole mile big!" he exclaimed.

We stopped at our fellow RHMA missionary's, Bill and Emma Horst, to spend the night. They lived near Intercourse, Pennsylvania, home of the horse-and-buggy Amish. All six of the kids sat on the porch watching the buggies go by, glued to the scene as if they were watching television. Bill and I taped some programs for the Horsts' radio program that went out over the south and the Caribbean, then Emma took us to their used clothing storage room. She outfitted all the kids with school clothes, jeans, and shirts, and gave Mari and Margie badly needed dresses. What a blessing!

By mid-September, it was already freezing. We concluded that we actually had only two seasons in the mountains—winter and the

Fourth of July. We still hadn't resolved our heating situation, and Bill kept busy hauling wood. Betty asked him to organize a wood bee for them since Winfield was still laid up with his broken back. The old nature in me wanted to tell her to go fly a kite, they could get their own wood just like she expected the preacher to do.

Bill, fortunately, was much more compassionate than his wife and dutifully tried to get the men together for a wood bee. Again, only Bill and George showed up. They worked hard all day to get enough wood to keep Betty and Winfield warm at least for a few weeks.

One of Bill's bosses from Caterpillar surprised us by sending a $400 check for our heat. "I'll send the rest of what you need in a couple of weeks," he wrote. Wow! With the stove paid for and the Oak Grove church promising to pay our monthly fuel bills, we thought God was telling us it was time for Bill to quit his job and begin trusting God again for our daily bread.

Before he turned in his notice, we bought half a beef for the freezer, 190 lbs. of meat, just in case our income dropped too drastically. Though it was only October, we also tried to get our Christmas shopping done for all the kids. We put some money in the bank to cover our income tax and county taxes, which would be higher because of the extra gifts we'd received for our heater and medical bills. Like squirrels piling up nuts for winter, we were getting prepared. Is that lack of faith, or what?

Another RHMA family wanted to buy our old wood heater, so Bill called a business meeting after church Sunday to discuss selling it. He suggested the church might want to keep it for future use, since it would be needed whenever we moved. What an uproar! The ones who were most adamant about not buying a furnace for the parsonage were highly indignant that we had the "audacity" to plan on taking our own oil heater with us. Our moving wasn't in question, but at that point, I think both Bill and I would have gladly packed our bags.

When the area RHMA "clan" came for the fellowship meeting at our house the next week, we joked and laughed about all of our struggles. It seems all the missionaries had gone to their churches on more than one occasion with a resignation letter in their pocket, but God usually stopped them from submitting it.

While we had never gone so far as writing a letter of resignation, there were times when we were strongly tempted. But giving up wasn't a part of Bill's M.O. With bulldog tenacity, he stayed by the stuff, preaching his heart out, showing love and compassion to his strongest detractors.

Winfield was in a large brace on his back, plus braces on his legs. He couldn't bend over at all, not even to dress himself, and it looked like he would probably be crippled the rest of his life. Their only son was hospitalized with an injury at the time Winfield fell, which meant they had no one to help. Bill used his last paycheck to buy bags of coal for them, in small enough bags for Betty to handle. Then he announced a "coal Sunday" at church, urging everybody to bring small bags of coal for Winfield and Betty. He was literally "heaping coals of fire!"

Wit-n-Wisdom: A critical tongue grows sharper with constant use.

CHAPTER 18

Staying by the Stuff

Therefore, my beloved brethren, be ye stedfast, unmoveable, always abounding in the work of the Lord, forasmuch as ye know that your labour is not in vain in the Lord. I Corinthians 15:58

With Bill home from work and able to stay with Jeff, I resumed teaching my Child Evangelism classes. The CE director asked me to add a club in Towanda in a strong Catholic neighborhood because of my experience working with Catholic kids in Milwaukee. The friend who had taken my class in Milan was unable to continue, so I took that one back. The director told us about a little shantytown near Powell, an old leather tannery factory housing, just loaded with children. They had tried to start a Good News Club there but couldn't find a home to host it. Would we be able to go down on Sunday afternoons and have a Sunday School in a rented building there?

Requests for piano lessons piled up, and I was trying to teach Margie and Mari to play. Billy was getting his musical training in the grade school band, and Johnny wasn't interested in anything musical, unless it was sung by a stock car racer. Teaching the Good News Clubs and piano students and working with the church youth group and missionary society filled every day of the week for me. Thankfully, most of my activities included our own kids, which meant I still was able to spend a lot of time with them. Driving to the various clubs and youth group activities produced some of our most precious family times away from the persistent phone calls and interruptions.

We took the young people's group on frequent trips to picturesque swimming holes, the Pennsylvania Grand Canyon, the Finger Lakes, Wyalusing Rocks, Watkins Glen, and other historic or scenic points of interest. Because our kids went with us, they got to see much of that part of the Endless Mountains.

I went calling every Tuesday evening with one of the ladies, and along with Bill's frequent visiting, the church began to grow. One Sunday we had so many strangers in church, Mabel Wilcox thought it was a pulpit committee from another church trying to steal Bill away.

Our Sunday School Annex was bursting at the seams. I promoted sixteen of my Beginners into the Primary Class, thinking I would have only four left in my class. The results of our visitation showed up that week, and I had a full classroom. Mabel Wilcox, the Primary teacher, was going in circles, trying to keep up with her huge new class. She had kids under the tables, on top the tables, all over the room. Some of the kids had to stand, and others were sitting on the floor. About that time, one of our friends resigned his church in Waverly and he and his wife decided to come to our church, with all eight of their children!

We had another baptismal service at Calvary Baptist in Athens— it was much too cold for an outdoor service. Bill was thrilled that his teaching was bearing fruit, especially among those who had refused to be baptized for years but who now saw the need to be baptized.

We had a successful Halloween party for the youth, with all sorts of hobgoblins and assorted spooks invading the "haunted" cellar of the Sunday School annex. Such screeching and hollering! When one little boy's parents arrived to pick him up, they asked, "Well, did you have fun?"

"Yup! I got all my pockets full!" he exclaimed, happily patting his pockets bulging with goodies.

We also enjoyed a record attendance at our annual Harvest Supper in East Smithfield. Church and Sunday School attendance continued to climb, packing the little church out Sunday after Sunday. Things were going so good, we decided to plan a trip to Illinois for Christmas, giving Margie and Johnny an opportunity to meet our relatives and friends back there.

But the devil wasn't about to give up without a fight, and we had six or seven folks in hospitals at the same time. Winfield lost all feeling in his feet, developed a bad infection in his toes that spread up his legs, and had to be hospitalized again. But, bless his heart, he didn't complain once through all the pain. He had such a great spirit about the whole ordeal, he was a joy to be around.

Our own heating problem was solved, much to Bill's doctor's delight. He didn't know, however, that Bill was continuing to chop and haul wood for Winfield and Betty. The first Saturday in November, he was out getting wood in the rain, snow, and wind and suffered another bout of heart failure, similar to what he had had the previous November.

I rushed him to the hospital, where they started him immediately on IVs and diuretic shots. They told me they could have him perking again very quickly. They did.

Sunday morning, he called from the hospital and told me to come pick him up after church. He was feeling extremely chipper and in good spirits, anxious to come home. While he was eating breakfast, however, he crumpled up and fell to the floor, unconscious. His left side was completely paralyzed, as well as his breathing muscles. A neurosurgeon "just happened" to be in the hallway when it happened and recognized it immediately as a stroke. Because they acted so quickly to dissolve the clot that had hit his brain, they didn't think Bill would have permanent damage.

By time I heard the news and drove up to the hospital, the paralysis had started to leave. His leg was normal and he could move his arm, but it was still limp. Late Sunday night, his facial muscles were still distorted and his speech slurred, but the doctors said this, too, would clear up rapidly.

The Bible says, "In all things give thanks." Yes, even in this, we had much to be thankful for. The doctor told me if Bill hadn't been in the hospital when the stroke occurred, he wouldn't have survived. But God, in His wisdom, got Bill to the hospital a day early! The doctors said the stroke was entirely unrelated to the mild heart failure they were treating him for.

As usual when we had troubles, I called Mom. She immediately made arrangements to arrive on the next train and became my stalwart for yet another hurdle.

After intensive physical therapy, Bill came home from the hospital, feeling very good. Too good, in fact. Both Mom and I tried to keep him down, but he just wouldn't, or couldn't, slow down. The doctors insisted that he stay in the house on complete bed rest for two weeks. I tried to make all his visits to keep him from worrying about people. We had seven people in area hospitals, plus a lot of house calls that needed to be made. I did a passable job of keeping up, while Mom kept the home fires burning. I also had my Bible clubs, which were growing rapidly, with twenty-three enrolled in Milan and thirteen in Towanda. Eight children made decisions for Christ that month, giving Satan another black eye.

One night we hosted the area pastors and wives for dinner. When they left, I had to rush up to the school to get in on the tail end of the kids' open house. We ran through the halls, trying to get to each kid's room before the teacher turned out the lights.

The hosting never seemed to let up, as people scheduled things at our house so Bill could be in on the event. Our new RHMA director and his family came up Sunday, so the other area missionaries came by, giving us another houseful of guests. On Thanksgiving, we had invited eighteen guests for dinner, an event we had planned long before Bill's stroke.

I wanted to cancel it and some of the other parties, but Bill wouldn't hear of it. He wanted to go ahead with everything. Usually a man of constant motion, he got awfully lonely and bored, pacing the floor with nothing to do. He couldn't even study very long, as he got terrific headaches when he read too much.

The stroke seemed to make some changes in Bill's personality, and he was more determined than ever to take care of us. One day while I was out cleaning house for one of our ladies who was coming home from the hospital with her new baby, Mom told me Bill sat and went through several catalogs, ordering expensive clothes for Mari, Margie, and me. She told him she knew we couldn't afford all that stuff, but he was insistent and completed the order. When he asked her to mail the order for him, Mom did something totally foreign to her. She slipped the envelope in her apron pocket to give to me later, walked out to the mailbox, and pretended to mail it.

Bill was equally determined to provide meat for the freezer, bought his hunting license, and prepared to tromp in the woods hunting for deer. I was worried sick that something would happen to him out in the woods alone and begged him not to go. But there was no stopping him. Late that afternoon he came home, deerless. "There's just no deer out there this year," he lamented.

Mom and I both laughed at him. "If you'd stayed home where you belong, you could have shot one from your recliner. Five deer, one a huge 12-point buck, sauntered through our yard this afternoon and came right up to the house!"

His health continued to improve and he looked like a physically fit athlete. The only residual damage from the stroke was to his vocal chords. He could speak clearly and distinctly, but his beautiful baritone singing voice was gone. He had sung solos over the years, thrilling us all with his anointed renditions of "Down from His Glory" or "No One Ever Cared for Me Like Jesus." With the annual Christmas program coming up, it was unlikely that we'd get to hear him sing the traditional "O Holy Night." I worked with him on arpeggios and vocal exercises, but the voice just wasn't there any more, a victim of the stroke.

The planned trip to Illinois was, of course, cancelled. The doctors said Bill's heart wasn't going to last much longer and scheduled open heart surgery at the University of Pennsylvania Hospital in Philadelphia sometime after Christmas. With the risky surgery hovering over us, we tried to make our holiday a happy one for the kids, determined not to think "doom and gloom."

And happy it was! No less than forty-five people sent us gifts of money, as did nine churches, Bill's former employer, and our own adult Sunday School class. The Windham-Summit and Bumpville churches had a huge grocery shower for us, Kennedy's Market gave us a lovely Christmas basket, the Good Neighbor Club had a grocery shower for us, and our Couples Club and missionary ladies both gave us Christmas baskets. We also received baskets from several individuals. The VIC class of the Sayre Baptist Church brought us a clever, and practical, money tree. God just overwhelmed us with loving friends and neighbors.

We put most of the money in the bank to use for our stay in Philadelphia, as we wouldn't have any income for a while. Vince Cooper, one of the men from Riggs who had recently resigned his pastorate, offered to pulpit supply while we were gone. We had enough food to last for a long, long time, including two turkeys and two canned hams. We were prepared for anything.

Farleys sent huge boxes of gifts for all of us, including Margie, Johnny, and Jerry, then thrilled us with a call from all the family back in Illinois while they were celebrating together. By time we passed the phone around several times so everybody could talk to everybody, we felt like we were part of the family Christmas party.

We had a lovely white Christmas, enjoying a big turkey dinner with just the eight of us. The girls washed the dishes, then we all gathered around the tree while Bill read the Nativity story from Scripture, with beautiful carols coming over his new FM radio (a gift from his folks).

Finally, the kids tore into their gifts from grandparents, uncles, and aunts. Each one had so many presents stacked in front of them it took most of the evening just getting them all opened. We did have time to try out the Twister game someone had sent. What a wild time that turned out to be! It got so rough, Bill tactfully suggested the girls and I should put on our new pajamas. He donned the matching pair he had received, so there we were, all duded up in gold pajamas with black polka dots, playing Twister. The kids laughed and laughed at Bill and me running around in matching PJs and told us we were too old to go steady.

On Christmas Day, we ate leftovers and enjoyed another quiet time at home. The roads were too bad to do much else. We did get out to church on Sunday, but not many made it. On Monday, the mail finally got through, bringing us yet another box full of wonderful gifts.

Bill's health fluctuated up and down through the holidays, with good days and bad days. After Christmas, I had to drive him to the hospital every day for diuretic shots. His liver was congested, and they were trying to clear it up. The Rehabilitation Department was taking care of all the details for his surgery, which they had told us would be some time between Dec. 18 and the first of February. The mantra for each day seemed to be "Hurry up and wait."

We kept Bill on a strict diet, and he lost a lot of weight. I also encouraged his exercise regime, and he was looking good. His office called and asked us to come up for a few minutes as they wanted to give him a gift. One of his former co-workers took one look at Bill and laughed. "Man, I should look so healthy! Are you sure you're sick?"

With his headaches getting better, Bill spent a lot of time reading. The Bible Lighthouse Bookstore gave us a number of books to help keep his mind occupied while we waited.

Finally, we got the word. Surgery was scheduled, and we should report to the University of Pennsylvania Hospital in Philadelphia Jan. 8. We enjoyed a wonderful time seeing the old year out at our second annual Watch Night Service. Our pastor friend, Rev. Marion Bell from Calvary Baptist in Athens, came down to provide music, and Rev. Vince Cooper, who would be our interim pastor during Bill's absence, did a chalk drawing.

Bill was able to have the communion meditation. What a precious time, spending the closing moments of 1966 fellowshipping around the Lord's table and hearing Bill open God's Word to us once again. We felt very close to our people, as well as to our friends at home who also were celebrating the Lord's Supper at that time.

The New Year started off with a BANG! I had to take Bill back to the local hospital Jan. 2, where he spent the week. The nurses rolled out the red carpet for their best customer and even talked of installing a pulpit for him. "He's always preaching to us anyway," they joked. "He might as well have a pulpit and be comfortable!"

After getting Bill situated at the hospital, I went home and literally conked out. Sometime Monday night, I fainted in the bathroom. Mom found me sprawled on the floor, my head on the heater. The next day, I entertained the flu bug, plus an ice bag for my aching head.

The unwelcome critter also visited Jeff and the girls, and the parsonage sounded like a sanitarium with all the coughing, sneezing, and whooping. We added another verse to the Old MacDonald ditty: "With a cough, cough here, and a cough, cough there—here a cough, there a cough; everywhere a cough, cough. All the Farleys had a cough, e-i-e-i-o!" By the end of the week, I told Satan, "Enough already! Go pick on somebody else for a while."

They released Bill from the hospital Friday afternoon, giving him a little time to spend with the kids before we were scheduled to leave for Philadelphia early Sunday morning. Marge Decker arranged with a friend of hers who lived in Philadelphia to pick us up; I was invited to stay at their house for the duration of Bill's hospital stay. Mom Crawford would stay with Billy, Mari, and Jeff to keep the home fires burning; Margie and Johnny went to stay with their grandmother until we returned from Philadelphia.

When Dan arrived Sunday morning to pick us up, it was no doubt the saddest day of our lives. Bill hugged Billy and Mari close to his chest, and I could only guess what was going through his mind. Would this be their last hug from their daddy?

Baby Jeff was still sleeping soundly in his crib. Not wanting to wake him, Bill reached down and stroked his head, choking back the tears. With a sob, he quickly left the room and headed for the car.

Wit-n-Wisdom: Faith draws the poison from every grief and takes the sting from every loss.

CHAPTER 19

Nyctophobia and Irrational Fears

For I reckon that the sufferings of this present time are not worthy to be compared with the glory which shall be revealed in us. Romans 8:18

We spent the five- or six-hour drive to Philadelphia getting acquainted with Dan and Jean Pomeroy, who would be my hosts for the next six weeks. They had joined a growing group of young professionals who were helping the city with a gigantic urban renewal program, buying historic row houses in the slums down by Dock Street.

Their house was still under renovation, as were many in the neighborhoods surrounding what is now Independence National Park. At that point in history, however, the area was very much a slum, with a random sprinkling of renovated row houses tucked in among the many boarded up ones.

We took Bill to the University Hospital near downtown Philadelphia and got him settled in his room. By then it was quite late, and driving through the bad parts of the city was an unsettling experience. The Pomeroys showed me the route I would have to walk each morning to catch a bus downtown. Their place was about six or seven blocks from the end of the bus route, which ended in Independence Square.

Walking through the slum area in the morning wasn't too bad, just a little scary. I was more concerned by the wind and blowing snow that blew off the nearby Delaware River. Philadelphia in January was not a pleasant place.

After spending the entire day with Bill, talking to doctors, and getting oriented to the hospital's routines, I ventured out again at 9 p.m. when visiting hours were over. And when the streets were frighteningly dark. As the bus ended its route, I glanced around and realized that I and one large man dressed in a dark trench coat were the only remaining passengers.

I got off the bus at the terminus, as did the man. I headed back over the route I had taken in the morning, hoping the man would head the other direction. He didn't. I increased my pace, scared of my own shadow by now. I hurried past boarded-up houses, graffiti-scarred buildings, and blocks of inner city ghetto trappings, my heart rate increasing with each hurried step.

Was he following me? Even if I yelled for help, there seemed to be no one in this deserted strip of city to hear my cry. Every time I turned a corner, my imagined assailant turned down the same street, walking close behind me, his head bent down into his coat collar to ward off the stinging wind. *Or to keep me from identifying him?* My fertile imagination worked overtime, and I had all but thrown myself into a major panic attack. *If that man doesn't get me, my pounding heart surely will!*

Relieved to see American Street was the next cross-street, I hurried my steps even more. Just six more row houses, and I'd be safe in my room. *Or would I? What if Jean and Dan weren't home and the man followed me in?* Satan had a field day, using my own wild imagination and fears to terrify me.

Just as I took the one step into our front door, the man passed by and smiled at me. "Good night," he called, as he mounted the steps to his own house, the Episcopal Church Rectory. Too late, I noticed the clerical collar beneath his coat. I could have enjoyed a pleasant walk with a fellow servant of God; instead, I allowed Satan to scare the socks off me!

I'd like to say I never feared the long walk through the ghetto each night for the next six weeks, but that wouldn't be true. I dreaded the nightly bus ride when often I was the only passenger and dreaded even more getting off the bus for the unnerving creepy walk home.

Daytimes were great. Bill and I spent a lot of quality time together, strolling through the hospital, sitting up on the roof deck when weather permitted, making dozens of new friends. On the days when he was scheduled for tests, I spent time in area museums and at historical sites, growing to love Philadelphia's rich history, before heading on over to be with Bill.

It was a teaching hospital, and because Bill's case was considered more or less experimental, he was often the "star" of the show. Large groups of medical students from around the country would come by, led by their instructors who discussed Bill's heart condition as if he weren't in the room. One in particular, a group from Duke University, surrounded Bill's bed while the professor droned on and on, pointing out the various parts of Bill's body to show the damage such a heart condition could do. He asked Bill to hold up his hand, then had each student individually rub the ridges on Bill's fingernails, almost like having them count the rings on a tree. "See," he pointed out. "This ridge shows a heart attack some months ago; this one is more recent...."

On a couple of occasions they wheeled Bill to a large theater, where he lay on a gurney while several doctors lectured huge groups of students. The nurses laughed each time they came to get him. "You have to be there or else the show can't go on!" they told him.

We looked forward to the daily mail drop from the Pink Lady. Every day one of the volunteers brought us a huge stack of mail, some from people we had never met. Especially heart-warming to us was the outpouring of love from people all over the country. Cards and letters from total strangers assured us they were praying for Bill, and his name was on dozens of prayer chains. Many wanted to know the exact day of surgery as they planned to spend the entire day in prayer vigils for him.

Because the heart-lung machine needed many pints of blood to keep it operating, we sent out a plea for blood donors. The East Peoria Jaycees sponsored a blood drive, resulting in 800 pints of blood. Several Bible colleges also held blood drives, as did our local blood bank in Athens and Sayre. The hospital staff actually requested that we ask the donations to stop because they had more blood than they could reasonably process.

Somehow people in a suburban Philadelphia church heard of our plight, sent a couple of deacons over to see us, and voila! many new friends. They took me on as their special project, picking me up for church services, making certain all my needs were met, and just being there for us both. Bill's cousin and her husband brought their pastor down from Detroit to pray with us, and some of our pastor friends drove down from northern Pennsylvania to encourage us.

Because Bill was under such watchful care, with a diet specifically designed for his metabolism and output, he felt better than he had in months. In some ways, our time together was almost like a second honeymoon, where we had time to sit and talk and dream. We discussed our future with the RHMA, laughing about the possibility of snagging a mission field somewhere warm, like Hawaii. "You can sit and write our prayer letters on the beach," Bill teased. "Tell them how we're suffering for Jesus, while I surf and soak up the sun."

Our "for real" prayer letter went out the first of February: *Greetings from Philadelphia, the city of brotherly love, polluted air and transit strikes!* Among details of Bill's health, we included this paragraph: *Although the waiting is hard, the bed rest has been good for Bill, and we know our Father has the times in His hands. Because of all the rest, Bill has had nearly 100% recovery from the stroke, except for his vocal chords—he can only sing in a monotone.*

The letter also had a note about our family: *Everything is fine on the home front. Jeff has the measles, but doesn't seem too sick. Our neighbors and church folks are being real good to Grandma Crawford and the kids—how we praise the Lord for them!*

As Bill and I discussed the future, we didn't spend much time worrying about the what ifs. But the possibility that Bill might not make it crept into our conversations occasionally. He tried to teach me to balance the checkbook, but as I'd learned during some of his other hospitalizations, mathematics and me were total strangers. "But you need to learn this, Dollie," he insisted. "What will you do if for some reason I don't make it through the surgery?"

Flippantly, I smarted off, "Well, I'll just go down to the bank and ask them to give me a joint account with some guy who's got money!"

"Come over here and apply that brain of yours to learning this," he said, beckoning for me to sit on the bed. "I don't want you getting overdrawn notices from the bank."

Playing the dumb blonde, I argued, "Well, if our bank sends me an overdrawn notice, I'll try some other bank. They can't all be overdrawn, can they?"

As usual, my zany antics sent us both into a laughing fit, and we ended up tussling on the bed. A nurse came in and frowned. "Whatever am I going to do with you two lovebirds?" she teased.

Bill spent a good deal of time witnessing and preaching to his nurses and roommates, all of whom changed shifts regularly. The nurses and interns were mostly students on rotation, while the other two beds in his room frequently changed occupants who came and went.

Bill was the only one who was consistent in his length of stay. The days became weeks, the weeks became a month, and it seemed like forever since we had seen our kids. We called them regularly and wrote to them often. Bill even drew pictures of trucks and cars for baby Jeff on postcards. We both missed the children dreadfully and looked forward to the times we could hear their voices on the phone.

One day, I was visiting the Liberty Bell while Bill was undergoing some tests. A woman stood near me, holding a little boy about Jeff's size. At that moment, I was overcome with such longing to hold my own baby that a literal physical pain ripped through my body. It felt like I was being torn apart from the inside out with a pain I had never experienced before or since.

Bill knew something was wrong the minute I stepped into his room. When I told him how much I missed Jeff, we both broke down and bawled. As soon as it was time for Billy and Mari to be home from school, we called home, just to hear their voices.

When we first arrived at the hospital, the doctors discovered that Bill's heart was so full of fluid that it was like a huge sponge covering most of his chest cavity. Obviously, they couldn't operate on it, so they put him on a new drug in an attempt to dry his heart out. Because the drug was still in the experimental stage, Bill became the proverbial guinea pig, getting stuck for so many blood tests and shots he looked and felt like a pincushion.

After six weeks of waiting for the doctors to get Bill healthy enough for the risky surgery, they came in and told us, "We're scheduling your surgery for Feb. 15."

We immediately called Dad and Mom Farley, who were already packed and ready to drive out to be with us for the ordeal. They arrived two days later, just in time to chat with Bill for a few minutes before the nurses came in and gave him medicine to help him get to sleep early to rest for his predawn wake-up time. The Farleys had rented a room in a boarding house not far from the hospital, and I elected to spend the night sleeping in a chair in Bill's room.

Tomorrow was the BIG DAY, the event around which our lives had revolved for the past twelve years. Tomorrow would begin a new chapter in our lives, one of serving the Lord with a new heart—at least a repaired one! I kissed Bill goodnight, than sat and held onto his hand as we both drifted off to dream about our wonderful new future.

Wit-n-Wisdom: It is good to learn of our weakness if it drives us to lean on His strength.

CHAPTER 20

The Waiting Game

Teach us to use wisely all the time we have. Psalm 90:12, CEV

The clock continued its relentless tick tock, tick tock. Eighteen long hours ago I had kissed Bill on the forehead and waved goodbye as the hospital orderlies wheeled his gurney down the long hall, into the elevator, and through the huge double doors marked "operating theater."

I knew what it would look like, with all its sterile surgical equipment, even the huge heart-lung machine that would pump gallons of blood through Bill's body as he lay motionless on the steel table, and his heart was removed from his body and held, literally, in the surgeon's hands. Two days previously, as part of our orientation for the open-heart surgery, hospital staff had given us a full tour of the facilities, trying to prepare us for what lay ahead.

They explained how they would place Bill on his stomach, cut through his back muscles and shoulder and remove his heart, letting the heart-lung machine keep him alive while his heart was repaired. Four teams of surgeons would alternate shifts of two or three hours each, with standby surgeons ready to step in if needed. They explained the probable hallucinations Bill would endure when he emerged from long periods of anesthesia-induced coma. And they tried to warn me how traumatic it would be to see him after surgery, with dozens and dozens of tubes protruding from his body, machines whirring around his bed, all of his bodily functions controlled by one apparatus or another.

Open-heart surgery was still in its infancy, and Bill was to be among the early experimental cases. The doctors prolonged such surgeries as long as possible, holding off the inevitable until it became a matter of life or death, only operating on patients for whom there was no other hope.

Knowing all this, our faith didn't falter. God was in control, and this was just one more hurdle to clear before we could get on with our ministry. God had great plans for our life. Once the heart surgery was behind us, we would have more energy and gusto to tackle our missionary endeavors.

Dad and Mom Farley sat with me in the surgical waiting room from about 5 a.m. All three of us stayed glued to our chairs, eyes on the door. Each time the door opened and a white-coated attendant entered, we simultaneously rose to attention, eager for news. Dad, a chain smoker, filled an ashtray with half-smoked cigarette butts, sometimes lighting another Camel before he'd finished the last one.

Someone kindly brought us snacks from the cafeteria, but we were all far too nervous to eat much. The interminable day went on and on. Mom drifted off to sleep, and Dad downed about half a dozen cups of coffee. I just sat there, praying and trying to will the clock hands to move faster.

Just before midnight, one of the heart surgeons came in, still clad in his operating room booties, bonnet, and smock coat. Pulling off his surgical gloves, he brushed his damp hair off his forehead and said, "We made it. He's in the recovery room now, and you should be able to see him in about an hour." He explained that the critical part was over. Bill's heart was back inside his body and beating regularly; he had survived the worst part. Now all we had to do was wait.

And wait we did. I spent the next two days and nights at Bill's bedside, leaving only to use the bathroom, or when the nurses ran me out of the room while they tended to Bill. Because of all the tubes, Bill couldn't speak, but he managed to write brief notes. One time when Dad entered the room, lit cigarette in hand, Bill became agitated, trying to communicate something. We couldn't understand his wild gestures and gave him a pencil and paper. "Oxygen on. Get that cigarette out of here!" he scrawled. Of course, posted all around were oxygen warning signs, but none of us had noticed them.

Bill continued to improve and didn't seem to be in much pain, except for his shoulder area where they had cut through the back muscles. Gradually the nurses removed one tube after another, leaving essential ones like the breathing apparatus and the ever-present heart monitor. My eyes were fixated on that monitor, watching his heart rhythms rise and fall with what looked like perfect regularity. The incessant tick tick of the monitor filled the room, and in the silence of night, it seemed to thunder. Even as I dozed in a chair by his bed, I could hear it as it permeated my subconscious mind with evidence that his heart continued to beat.

By Friday evening, his condition improved so much they removed him from the "critical" list and changed his status to "guarded." They helped him sit up in bed and brought him a turkey sandwich—the first real food he had enjoyed in days. He was feeling so good, the nurses urged me to go with Bill's folks to the boarding house and get some rest. "He'll be fine. He's doing great," they assured me. For the first time that week, I left the hospital.

About 2 or 3 a.m., I heard the phone ringing at the boarding house. Our hostess knocked on the bedroom door and whispered, "It's the hospital, calling for you."

I reached for the phone with shaking hand. "You need to come as soon as possible. He's taken a turn for the worse, and we don't think he's going to make it." I was trembling so much I could barely get my clothes on in our rush to the hospital.

The sight that met our eyes that night is one I'll never be able to blank out of my memory. They had hooked Bill back up to much of the equipment they had removed. My beloved, who had seemed so cheerful and raring to go just a few hours earlier, lay helpless in a coma, his eyes darting wildly about the room. The doctor was kind, but his concern showed on his face as he told me, "His heart has stopped several times this morning, and there really isn't much hope. We're doing everything we know how to do, but I'm afraid it's entirely up to God."

The doctors assured me Bill was unconscious and unaware of anything, but they cautioned us to be careful what we said, as "hearing is the last sense to shut down." As the doctors worked frantically to restore Bill's heartbeat, I sat by his bed, rubbing his arm, holding his hand, desperate to bring life back to his body.

With the aid of all the machinery, his heart resumed beating, and the monitor began its steady "click, click, click." I breathed deeply. *He was going to make it. He had to. He wasn't even 32 years old…. Nobody dies that young. Besides, we had lots of ministry left to do. Bill's got many years of service left.*

All day the doctors and technicians worked with Bill; all day I sat by his side, willing him to wake up and talk to me, to assure me he was going to make it. I told him how much I loved him, how much he meant to me and the kids, how much we needed him. *"Please come back to us,"* I begged.

He endured several more episodes where his heart stopped. Each time, the doctors were able to shock it back into rhythm. Late in the afternoon, his body suddenly lurched in the bed, and the doctors asked me to leave the room while they continued to work on him. They sent me down the hall to the waiting room, where Bill's folks were nervously keeping vigil.

I hugged Mom and told her Bill was going to be OK. "We've just got to keep trusting God," I encouraged her.

Once again, the clock on the wall took center stage as I continued waiting. Every few minutes, I was drawn back to Bill's room. I couldn't get in because of all the activity, but sometimes I managed to get a peek into the room. I found some comfort just in being close to him.

"While there's life, there's hope," I consoled myself over and over again. Desperately I searched the Scriptures for something to hang on to. And there in the Psalms, I found it: *Because he hath set his love upon me, therefore will I deliver him....with long life will I satisfy him, and shew him my salvation.*

What a promise! What a comfort! I showed the passage to Mom, assuring her that God was speaking to us and telling us not to worry.

As more minutes pushed more hours into the pages of eternity past, I clung frantically to those promises in Psalms 91. Even with so little hope, God was going to perform a miracle. Just like Christ had allowed Lazarus to die to bring greater glory to God, Bill was being taken right to the point of death, so that his healing would be an even greater miracle. Bill WOULD live, I had no doubt about it.

It was easy to pray "Thy will be done" because I was so positive that God's will and mine were one and the same. As Bill had so often joked, "I'm indestructible until my job on earth is done."

After many more torturous hours of waiting, Dr. Noon appeared at the waiting room door and beckoned me. Trembling, I rose slowly and followed him into the hall, where he gave me the life-shattering words, "I'm so sorry, Mrs. Farley. We've done everything we can, but it isn't enough. Bill's brain is showing no activity, and we need your permission to shut off the machines that are keeping him breathing."

Numbly, I took the pen he offered and signed the permission slip on the clipboard he extended toward me.

Dr. Noon gave me a compassionate hug. "I'm so sorry," he consoled me, tears brimming his eyes. "I really thought he was going to make it." He told me it would take a few minutes to get the machinery cleared from the room. "I'll send a nurse to get you when we're done," he promised. "Feel free to sit with him as long as you'd like."

A few minutes later, I made my way down the hall, quietly following the nurse who had come for me. Dr. Noon's message was not registering in my brain. Bill wasn't gone—I couldn't make myself even think the word "dead." God would still send that miracle. A nurse would detect a faint heartbeat, the monitor would begin ticking; somehow, someway, Bill was still alive. It would be a miracle like no one had ever seen before, bringing great glory to God. The news would spread rapidly among all those around the country who were at this moment praying for Bill. What a day of rejoicing we would all enjoy!

I entered his room with great anticipation, my eyes drawn to the man on the bed. He lay unmoving, all the tubes removed, no monitors, no IVs, no tracheotomy. A few minutes earlier, the room had been utter chaos; now a sense of absolute peace encircled the room and covered Bill's face.

Trance-like, I took the chair next to the bed and reached for Bill's hand. Cold and hard, it felt nothing like Bill's warm, comforting hand—the hand he had so often used to playfully ruffle my hair, pat my back, or put cold cloths on my forehead when I was sick.

I couldn't breathe. He was gone. Really and totally gone. I laid my head on his chest and wept, letting the tears flow unchecked. *God, where are You? What about all those promises in Your Word?* In the stillness, God reminded me of our last prayer letter, where we had so boldly declared, *Though He slay me, yet will I trust Him.*

"Can you still trust me?" God seemed to whisper to me. "Even in this?"

Mom and Dad Farley joined me in the room, and we all said our final goodbyes to their much-loved son and my beloved husband of twelve years. In a fog, I somehow went through the process of making arrangements for Bill's body to be shipped back to Illinois, securing a local funeral director, and getting him in touch with the funeral home in East Peoria that would handle Bill's final services.

Before we could leave the hospital, I had to check out through the cashier's department to settle payment plans for the huge bills I knew we had run up. Six weeks in the hospital, operating room fees, all those numerous surgeons, the amazing equipment costs—I knew I'd be paying off medical bills for the rest of my life. But God showed me right then how He was worthy of my complete trust and confidence. The cashier expressed her condolences (it seems everyone in the hospital had known about Bill's condition) and handed me a check for $32. "Your bill has been paid in its entirety," she said. "In fact, you have a small credit coming back to you."

We never learned who paid the bill, but we rejoiced in God's goodness. It seemed as if God was telling me He would be there for us no matter what happened; I needn't worry about our future.

I faced the unpleasant task of calling my mom and the kids with the terrible news, and we had to prepare to drive home from Philadelphia yet that night. I was especially concerned how the kids would take the news. Mari had great faith that God was going to heal her daddy and was eagerly waiting for our return home. What would this do to her childish faith? God had failed to answer her prayers on such an important matter, would she continue to believe in a loving God?

I quickly phoned the news to Mom, who took the kids in her arms and gave them the bad report. Mom told me later that Billy immediately broke into wrenching sobs, but Mari just got quiet and went into her room. She finally came out, a radiant smile on her face. "I've been praying that God would make Daddy well," she said. "And He has. He made Daddy well forever. He'll never be sick again."

The next few days passed in a blur. The long-awaited post surgery days we had anticipated vanished into a quagmire of funeral arrangements, packing to move back to Illinois, and dozens of folks dropping by the parsonage to bring food and give their condolences.

The Farleys and I arrived back in Riggs late Saturday night, where the kids embraced me tearfully. It was then I was struck by the awesome realization that I was now their only parent, totally responsible for their security. Despite the emotional upheaval of the past few weeks, I hugged my three precious children and vowed to do everything in my power to take care of them. For their sake and for Bill's sake, I would see that they continued to trust in Jesus so they could be reunited with their daddy one day in Heaven.

Mom had prepared our upstairs bed for Dad and Mom Farley, anticipating they would stay through Bill's local memorial service, which the church had already scheduled for Tuesday.

I slept on the couch in the living room, and sometime during the night woke up screaming, "It's started! They got Bill's heart started again!" Mom came rushing out of Mari's room to see what was going on. She found me sobbing and trying to stop the alarm clock I'd placed by the couch. Its constant "tick tick, tick tick" had penetrated my subconscious, triggering memories of the incessant ticking of Bill's heart monitor. For years after that, I couldn't sleep with a clock ticking anywhere within hearing distance.

As we prepared for church the next morning, Dad shocked us all. "We're leaving this morning," he announced. My mom and Bill's mother both pleaded with him to stay and help with the packing, but he was adamant. "I said we're leaving, and we're leaving!" Turning to Mom Farley, he told her, "Get your suitcases packed back up and let's get out of here."

On the drive up from Philadelphia, I had sensed his anger, but I didn't quite know what to make of it. He was obviously angry at me and especially at our church people. He was barely civil to those who stopped by to offer condolences. "Those folks don't deserve to have a memorial service!" he told me. Normally a friendly, cordial man, Dad's anger was uncharacteristic and unexplicable.

My mom, whom I'd never heard utter an angry word in her life, turned on him. "How can you just go off and leave Dollie and the kids here to face this alone?" she demanded. "What kind of man would do that to a widow and her children? And how is she going to drive all the way back to Illinois without your help?"

But he had stubbornly set his mind on going. A few minutes later, they left for Illinois. My mom, still explosive with anger, muttered, "Well, good riddance!"

Not quite the peaceful atmosphere one would expect in the parsonage, but it was one brought on by weeks of stress and uncertainty. Eventually I learned that anger is one of the first stages of grief for most people, and Dad was deeply grieving the loss of his son. He later tried to make up for his insensitivity and was a tremendous help to me and the kids for the rest of his life, a grandpa we all loved dearly.

We spent all day Monday packing to move. Grief counselors tell widows not to do anything hastily and to stay in their current home for at least a year. That's ordinary widows. Pastors' widows have to move immediately to make room for the next pastor's family. Our folks were very gracious and told me to take my time, but I knew the church needed a new pastor immediately to keep the ministry going smoothly and the RHMA already had someone in mind to take our place.

The day Bill died, an area missionary couple was killed in a car crash. Three of God's choice young servants were called Home that Saturday. The Christian radio station in Montrose, WPEL, devoted its broadcast all day Sunday as a memorial to the three popular Christian workers. The news of Bill's death spread throughout the valley, and we knew his memorial service would be highly attended.

Calvary Baptist Church in Athens offered its much larger sanctuary for Bill's service, and four of our pastor friends conducted the service. An open mike was passed around for people to share their memories of Bill. It was a very emotional time. One of our deacons, the man who had given us so much grief in recent months, shook as he took the mike. "We've driven out every pastor we've ever had," he said, sobbing hard. "When we were so mean and ornery to Mr. Farley, he just kept loving us anyway—and now God has taken him away from us!"

The service lasted so long we decided to start our long drive back to Peoria the following day, giving us just two days to get back in time for Bill's visitation. The van loaded with everything we could possibly pack in, we said goodbye to a way of life we had come to love. Margie and Johnny had gone to stay with their grandmother while Bill and I were in Philadelphia; now we had to leave them behind permanently. They had become so much a part of our family, like brothers and sisters to our kids, the parting was sorrowful. We also found good homes for our pets, but it was still hard on Mari and Billy to give them up.

Amidst all the trauma of parting, we started out early Wednesday morning. Mom didn't drive, but she was my co-pilot, reading maps and road signs like an expert. Another nasty storm blew in over the Great Lakes, making the roads nearly impassable for mile after endless mile.

Late that night, we pulled into a motel to try to get some rest, and Mom literally had to pry my tightly clenched fingers off the steering wheel. My back was so tense I couldn't straighten up and nearly had to crawl into the motel room. Except for our tedious drive back from conference the previous year, I had never driven for more than an hour or so, just enough to give Bill a rest from driving. Now it was over 800 miles of wind, snow, and ice.

Conditions continued to get worse and worse, forcing us to spend a second night in a motel, meaning we would get to Peoria just in time for the visitation if we were lucky. I called Dad Farley from a pay phone, and he said he'd taken care of all the funeral arrangements back there, so all we had to do was show up.

That wasn't as easy as it sounded, however. Coming down Route 66, we hit a real blizzard and could barely see the road. The blowing, drifting snow picked up the black dirt that made Illinois farms famous, packing it onto our headlights so thick that Billy, now the man of the house, had to keep getting out to scrape it off. In just those few minutes, his face was totally blackened, and I had to dig the sticky black stuff out of his ears.

Conditions got so bad the Illinois State Police closed the roads at Chenoa. We pulled into a Stuckey's Restaurant parking lot, joining hundreds of other stranded travelers to wait out the storm, knowing that if we had to stay too long, we'd never make it in time for the visitation.

When hearing of our plight, a friendly trucker offered, "I'm heading down Route 24 and have to get through tonight. If you trust me, just follow my tail lights and I'll get you through."

So for mile after mile, we followed what we could see of his red taillights, which looked like a tiny dot on the horizon in the blowing snow. We had no idea if we were still on the highway or in a farmer's field; if we were going through a town or running stop lights. The only thing we could see was that tiny red dot. By time we got to Washington, just a few miles from home, the storm stopped. Dad Farley thought I was grossly exaggerating how bad it had been. "Clear as a bell here," he insisted.

So many people tramped into Schmidt's new funeral parlor for the visitation, the owner actually went downstairs to check the floor trusses. He had never had a crowd so large and wanted to make sure the floor would hold up.

Home at last, we still had some major obstacles to contend with. The temperature dropped to 25 below zero, and the cemetery sexton wasn't sure if they could even dig Bill's grave in the frozen ground. They decided to tent the area that night and install a heat blower to thaw the ground enough to open the grave.

On my 30th birthday, Feb. 25, 1967, we had Bill's funeral. Our home church pastor, Gary Hansen, and several other area pastors conducted the services and huge crowds braved the bitter cold to pay their respects. While many of us went to the cemetery for the burial, the ladies from our home church went to Mom Crawford's house to prepare the meal for everyone. They offered to keep Jeff and the Hansen's little boy at Mom's house with them.

God gave me strength to get through the ordeal as I stood and greeted the hundreds of friends and relatives, even though my back was aching from the stressful trip. God kept me calm and surrounded me with His peace in a manner I can't describe. The only point where I nearly lost control was in the kitchen at Mom's, when someone exclaimed, "Oh, here comes your daddy!" She was speaking to the Hansen's little boy, but when 18-month-old Jeff heard "Daddy," he ran to the door, eagerly yelling, "Daddy! Daddy!" The disappointment on his face when he discovered it wasn't his daddy was more than any mother should have to see.

We eventually bought an old farmhouse just across the lane from Mom's house, and I went to work in the RHMA office as promotional secretary. God continued to provide our daily needs and, as He promised, became a father to the fatherless. Never once did He let us down, and though the road I walked was often a lonely one, God was always by my side, leading and comforting.

Wit-n-Wisdom: The value of life lies not in the length of days, but in the use we make of them...Montaigne

Epilogue

Thou art the helper of the fatherless. Psalms 10:14

Was it worth it? For three short years, we ministered in one of America's poverty pockets, a place most would consider too small to bother with. But in God's perfect timing, He sent the RHMA and our family to Riggs to keep a tiny church from closing its doors.

In the course of those three years, more than sixty people came to know Christ, and at least ten young people went into full-time Christian service under Bill's ministry. The church that struggled so hard just to stay alive received a new lease on life. In place of the ramshackle little meeting house we worshipped in, Grace Baptist Church now has a beautiful new building with no mortgage, and a thriving congregation continues to bring light to the valley.

Bill's short ministry was a tremendous blessing, not only to the members of the small churches he served and the many people he won to the Lord, but to the scores of people who witnessed his faith and courage in the face of seemingly insurmountable obstacles.

Because of Bill's witness, a young couple, the parents of eight children, sold their business and enrolled at Tennessee Temple to prepare for ministry, a discouraged pastor stayed on at his problem-racked church, a heart specialist left a thriving practice to serve in the slums of Philadelphia. Countless others responded in less spectacular ways. Seeing God work in Bill's life gave added impetus to the faith of many who were struggling.

Two men who had been his roommates in the hospital both accepted Christ, saying, "We couldn't figure out why God would take a great, young guy like Bill, and let us two old geezers live. Then we realized he was ready to go, and we weren't. So we want what he had."

One of Bill's biggest concerns as he waited for the surgery was, "What's going to happen to our kids? How can you take care of them alone if I don't make it?" We comforted ourselves with the confidence that God would care for the kids, that God Himself would be their father if He chose to take Bill home.

And what a great job He did! Two years after Bill's home going, God brought another preacher into our lives, a widower with four young children of his own. We merged our two families, went to Idaho as rural missionaries, and later became general director of Missionary Gospel Fellowship in California. We marvel as we look back and see God's plan every step of the way. As Jimmy Stewart said, "It's a wonderful life!"

Billy graduated from John Brown University with a bachelor's in music education, then went on to get a master's and a doctorate from Covington Theological Seminary. He was ordained to the ministry and serves in rural Idaho with the Missionary Gospel Fellowship and is choral director for the South Fremont School District.

Mari graduated with highest honors from Moody Bible Institute, completed her bachelor's in communications at John Brown University, and earned master's degrees in journalism and history at the University of Arkansas. The author of several books, Mari was a contributing author to Zondervan's *Grandmother's Bible*.

Jeff attended John Brown University, served four years in the Marines, and earned his bachelor's in criminal justice from a northern California university. A detective for the Sacramento County Sheriff Department, Jeff teaches juniors at his church and directs their summer Sports Camp. True to Bill's original nickname for him, "Little Thumper" is president of the River Valley Falcons football league and also serves as a football coach.

All three have loving Christian spouses and children of their own. It's exciting to see God working in the next generation as they serve the Lord with gladness. Bill didn't live to see his three kids grow up; he didn't get to meet his eight grandchildren or five great-grandchildren.

But I like to think Bill is in that "great cloud of witnesses" that Hebrews 12 mentions, up there in Heaven cheering us on, rooting for us, and waiting for that Glad Reunion Day.

Our children have been blessed more abundantly than we could ask or think. God gave them a very special biological father, then sent them the world's best second father to take over where Bill had to leave off. We chose never to use the word "stepfather" or "stepdad" in our house. Bill was their father who lived in Heaven with Jesus, Jack was their Dad to guide them through life here on earth, and God was our Heavenly Father who loved and cared for us all.

Wit-n-Wisdom: "God will not permit any troubles to come upon us, unless He has a specific plan by which great blessing can come out of the difficulty"—Peter Marshall

About the Author

Bill and Adell "Dollie" Farley experienced hand-to-mouth living in one of JFK's poverty pockets in northern Appalachia during the 1960s, living "from God's hand to their mouths." As faith missionaries with very little monthly support, the family of four learned how to literally depend upon God for their daily bread, the doctor bills, and the bare necessities of life.

Bill, an engineer for a large manufacturing company, and Dollie, an executive secretary for the same company, spent the first nine years of their married life in relative affluence, enjoying a lovely home and lifestyle in central Illinois. Then God called them to become rural missionaries in the Endless Mountains of Pennsylvania. For the next three years, the Farley family struggled with Bill's deteriorating heart condition, learning a new culture, pastoring a country church, and financial hardships. Tucked away in the mountain hamlet during the turbulent sixties, they lived an exciting life, making themselves available to God and watching Him perform miracle after miracle. Each time a new problem sprung up, they answered it with a question: "Okay, God, how are You going to handle this one?"

Dollie wrote weekly letters to their parents back in Illinois detailing God's amazing provision, sometimes griping about the hardships, and giving her daily perspective of events as they happened. Both Bill's mother and Dollie's mother kept all these letters, which were found in their homes when they died.

The letters provided an accurate description of emotions and events, assuring that long-ago memories are true accounts of what actually happened, a weekly journal that Dollie used as the basis to reconstruct a memoir of those three exciting years.

When Bill died following open heart surgery in 1967, God did not abandon the family. Dollie and their three children returned to Illinois, where God later "merged" her family with a well-to-do widower and his four. God blessed the merger with an eighth child, making the Harvey-Farley Gang a "yours, mine, and ours" tribe. Their exploits are chronicled in Dollie's first humorous book, *My Cope Runneth Over* (Thos. Nelson Publishers).

The Harvey-Farley gang also answered God's call to rural America, selling their electrical contracting business and moving to Idaho as missionaries to the Mormons. In 1995 Jack was asked to become General Director of Missionary Gospel Fellowship in Turlock, California, and Dollie tagged along as office manager. When Jack stepped down from his executive position in 2003, the Harveys became public relations directors for the mission. They continue to serve on the leadership team of MGF and as facilitators for the Punjabi and Hispanic ministries in Yuba City, California. Jack and Dolllie are also VBS leaders for the Sierra Butte Baptist Association of thirty churches in northern California. In the midst of ministry, raising eight kids, spoiling sixteen grandkids and six "greats," Dollie has authored fourteen books.

CPSIA information can be obtained at www.ICGtesting.com
Printed in the USA
269147BV00001B/1/P